GHOSTS OF
THE KLONDIKE

THEY HAUNT THE FROZEN NORTH

GHOSTS OF THE KLONDIKE

THEY HAUNT THE FROZEN NORTH

By Shirley Jonas

Illustrated by Chris Caldwell

LYNN CANAL PUBLISHING
Skagway, Alaska

ISBN: 0-945284-04-7

Direct inquiries to:
Lynn Canal Publishing
P.O. Box 1898, 264 Broadway
Skagway, Alaska 99840-0498
Phone 907-983-2354
Fax 907-983-2356
E-mail: skagnews@ptialaska.net

Printed In U.S.A.

Lovingly dedicated to the late Harold Sherman and to his lovely wife Martha in Mountain View, Arkansas.

~~~

Energy and matter can not be destroyed, only transformed. We are the energy and we are forever!

~~~

And to my grandchildren, who listened!

~~~

My heartfelt thanks also go to my editors, publishers and good friends, Jeff and Diane Brady. Without their encouragement, patience and enthusiasm, this book might still be stacks of notes and tapes on my cluttered desk.

CONTENTS

Foreword

I remember thinking how incongruous it was, that I was kneeling on cold rocks on the edge of a stream on the Chilkoot Trail, contemplating what little I knew of Einstein's philosophy. Specifically, that nothing is ever destroyed; that matter becomes energy and vice-versa.

Watching the water flow from my filter-pump into the hiking cannister, I was trying to sort out a discussion I had just had with my sister, Shirley Jonas, regarding the nature of ghosts. She, our other sister Bobbie, and I were hiking the trail for the pleasure of the trip and also to go along with her while she "chased ghosts," or at least ghost stories.

Shirley had invited me to come to her Skagway, Alaska home and then on up to Dawson City and beyond, while she continued her research for this collection of tales and reminiscences. Our two-part adventure became an extraordinary vacation in which, although not traveling on the Yukon River between Whitehorse and Dawson City, we covered the same terrain as the gold seekers of 1898. There was much to learn and more to ponder on the way.

Somewhere between Sheep Camp and the Scales at the base of the Chilkoot Pass, I found a boulder to rest on a few feet off the trail. Sitting there, I saw in the bushes, an old, upright, rough, wooden cross with a bleached bit of canvas nailed where a name plate would have been. I called out, "Look!" to some people hiking by. They were nearly trotting, and only nodded and kept on. They could not have seen the cross. "Target people," the rangers call them. All muscle, no eyes. So I thought about that too. Maybe most of us are target people, at least to the degree that we are insensitive to other beings that may inhabit the same space we are in, but not the same time.

On the long, downward, snow-covered slope into Canada, after passing over the crest of the much-photographed "Golden Stairs," we leaned our packs against the crib built to hold the tramway cable erected in 1899. Twenty-foot logs are stacked slate-like to hold a fifteen-foot-high square basket of boulders, like a giant's shoe box of marbles. Even more than shovels, shoes and saddle bags seen along the way, this structure on the treeless slope speaks of the stamina of the people who built it. Perhaps it is this tremendous strength of spirit that will not go away and becomes "ghosts?"

I don't know. Shirley and I talked about it over tea, sitting by campfires, while gathering wild onions along the shore of Lake Laberge, and in the old van as we forded streams and bumped over the road built on piles of tailings at Sixty Mile. And even though she has much more knowledge of the paranormal than I, due to years of study, she didn't push a theory or discourage my musings.

She conducted interviews in the same open and encouraging way, allowing people to just simply tell what they had experienced. I think these stories reflect that and are thereby more interesting and insightful.

One of my favorite snapshots from the trip is of Shirley, placing flowers on John Stockton's grave. She writes of that moment in "The Perpetual Prospector." It was such a natural thing for her to do. Loving and respectful. And I believe that in itself is a statement of how she feels about ghosts, along the Klondike trail or anywhere.

Regretfully, there was not enough space or supportive information yet for Shirley to include many of the stories she heard. One I personally want to know more about are the screams and voices heard by rangers on the Chilkoot near Sheep Camp late in the season as they are closing down the camp and evenings are long and quiet. Another is the wraith of a woman who stands near a gate on land across the Yukon River from Dawson City.

Well, another time . . . .

Frances A. Turney
Anchorage, Alaska

SKAGWAY, ALASKA

"Mary"

The Moveable Ghost and Other Hauntings of the Golden North Hotel

If there ever was a "gaggle of ghosts" (or should I say — "giggle?") in one building, that's the Golden North Hotel!

They glide down the halls, sit on your bed, attempt to choke you in the middle of the night, and, last but not least, they stand dazzling in light in the doorways for hours. The stories are many. Some a little hard to believe, but nonetheless, extremely interesting.

It took a little while to trace down the story of "Mary," who is the most famous "guest" of the Golden North Hotel. She has been seen by many, from the employees of the hotel to so-called "no-nonsense" guests, such as a couple of construction workers who checked out of their room faster than they checked in. Or was it really Mary they saw? We'll get into that later.

The mystery in tracing Mary took at least a couple of months to solve and a lot of "digging," if you'll pardon the expression.

3

The story goes that Mary died in Room 24 in the Golden North in 1898, but this just didn't add up for a while. For the present Golden North, at that time, was not a hotel at all, but the Klondike Trading Company.

Two blocks away, on the corner of Third and State Streets, the Klondike Trading Company early in 1898 built a two-story wood building with an onion tower. After the stampede for gold slowed down somewhat, this building was rented by the Army as barracks until 1904.

George Dedman and Edward Foreman purchased the Klondike Trading Company building and in 1908-1909 had it moved to the southwest corner of Third and Broadway, where it stands today. They added a third floor, raised the corner dome another story, and refitted the structure as a hotel. They named it the Golden North.

So, if Mary died in 1898, where did she spend those last moments? The popular story told that she passed away in the Golden North. How could this be if the hotel didn't exist in 1898?

Frank Norris, a National Park Service historian, helped me unravel the mystery. He managed to locate a map of Skagway that was printed in 1910. Lo and behold, on this map we found a hotel on Fourth between State and Main that was named (you guessed it) The Golden North Hotel. The original Golden North was open for business during the time of the gold rush, however it was torn down near the time that the new Golden North was opened. Dedman and Foreman also were owners of the old Golden North.

4

It is not at all unusual for a ghost to move from one structure to another, especially if the structure is owned by the same people and bears the same name.

One such case as this took place in York, England. A theater had burned down and supposedly the famous ghost went to its final rest in the fire. Not so! When the theater was re-built two blocks away, the same ghost showed up in the new building.

So it's quite possible that Mary's ghost just moved from one Golden North to the other.

Legend has it that Mary was a young woman of eighteen and came to Skagway after receiving a letter from her fiance. He had written to her saying that he had "struck it rich" in the Dawson gold fields and would she meet him in Skagway where they could be married. Mary, who was a courageous lady and as full of adventure as her fiance, packed up her personal belongings, including a beautiful lace wedding dress, and arrived in Skagway to wait for the man she loved.

Alas, her husband-to-be never returned.

There are many stories about the prospectors who died along the treacherous "Trail of '98." Some perished in disastrous snow slides like the one that killed seventy-three people at the base of the Chilkoot Pass on Palm Sunday, April 3, 1898. Others drowned in the icy waters of Lake Bennett or the Yukon River after being spilled from their make-shift rafts and boats, or perished in the sub-zero temperatures on the winter trail to Dawson City and the Klondike gold fields.

No one will ever know what happened to Mary's

fiance, but the story came back that he died along the trail in a dog sled accident.

Mary refused to believe that she had lost the man she loved. Not long after this, she became mortally ill from tuberculosis — what they called consumption in those days. The proprietor of the hotel at that time discovered her lying peacefully on her bed in her lace wedding gown. Mary had died sometime during the night.

It is said that Mary is a peaceful, unpretentious spirit, never purposely frightening anyone. There have been times when she has tried to communicate with guests in the hotel. Two, in particular, who stayed in Room 13, were cousins: one from Whitehorse, Canada, and the other from New York. In the middle of the night, one of the ladies felt someone sit down on her bed. She sat up to see if it was her cousin, thinking that she might not be well, and found that her cousin was in the other bed sound asleep! She watched as the depression on her bed disappeared, and the feeling of a presence left the room.

Staff and guests of the hotel have reported seeing the graceful form of a young woman in a long white gown appear to them in the hallway of the third floor near Room 24, where Mary was supposed to have died, as well as in rooms on the second floor. They have also said that they have heard footsteps in the night going down the long carpeted hallways and a rustling sound quite similar to that of an old-fashioned petticoat under a long gown. But when they quickly looked, no one was there.

Perhaps Mary's gentle spirit is still waiting for her wedding day?

If Mary is a gentle spirit, then what was it, or who was it that appeared to Sharon and John Garland.

The story Sharon Garland told me was enough to raise the hair on the nape of your neck. Sharon is the owner of the Forget-Me-Not gift shop next to the Golden North Hotel. Seated in her cozy office in the back of the gift shop, she told me the following story. And I would like to pass it on to you, almost word-for-word. For I could not tell it any better than Sharon:

"This was back in 1983 in the winter. My husband John worked on the pipeline for a number of years. I was living in Juneau with my children. I'm a believer in ghosts and just about anything supernatural. I don't believe that these things are all good. I think there is a lot of evil and we have to be very careful. Anyway, John was coming home from the north for a little 'R and R' from the pipeline. This was about Christmas time. While in the Anchorage airport, he picked up a newspaper and in it was a story about the ghost of the Golden North Hotel in Skagway. In the meantime, I had picked up the newspaper in Juneau — I believe it was the Empire — and there was the same story! I cut it out and saved it, and when John walked in the door he handed me the story from the Anchorage paper, saying 'Here's something about that ghost in Skagway. Thought you might be interested.'

"John is a skeptic. He believes in absolutely nothing that can't be nailed down! We sat down and talked about the ghost, and I said to him, 'Let's go to Skagway. You have five days of 'R and R.' Let's go and take the kids and stay in the Golden North Hotel!

"So I called the Golden North to make reservations. It was the dead of winter, between Christmas and New Years, and very cold! At that time the road to Whitehorse was closed for the winter and Skagway was not the bustling tourist town that it is in the summer. I told the hotel that we were a family of five and we would like to stay in the 'ghost room.' I was told that, in the winter, the third floor was closed off and not heated, but we could stay on the second floor. So I said okay — we'll take anything we can get!

"We took the ferry from Juneau to Skagway, a six-hour trip. But the Alaska ferries are very big and comfortable and we had a wonderful trip talking about Mary the ghost, and what we might find when we got there.

"The ferry arrived in the middle of the night, but the owner of the hotel, Donna Whitehead, was there to meet us in the hotel van. We had never been to Skagway, so we were very excited about the whole trip. The winter sky was ablaze with northern lights, and on the dock there were some kind of chains or loose metal banging in the wind. It was very windy that night. The hotel was dark except for the lobby, and the streets were deserted. There wasn't anyone checked into that big hotel except us, and of course, the Whitehead family who resided there. It was just wonderful! The setting was perfect. We were on a ghost hunt and it was just perfect!

"So, we checked in and went to bed. The high wind whistled around that old building, rattling the windows, and it was rather eerie. But we snuggled down and went to sleep, warm and cozy. We were in Room 14, which is an elegant room, all done in blue. And the kids were down the hall in Room 12. We were very impressed with this big, beautiful old hotel. There were no occurrences that night. If there had been, we were too sound asleep to hear or feel anything.

"The next day we spent time sight-seeing, and that night we went to an alumni game at the high school. I walked back to the hotel with my family, and we all checked into our rooms. John and I were starting to get ready for bed, and we were discussing how wonderful it was to be in Skagway. We had really fallen in love with this place, and we were so excited about the possibility of seeing the ghost that night. John was joking, but I was serious! Just before we went to our rooms, Luke Whitehead had taken us up to the third floor. The only light we had was his flashlight. There was a wooden door, locked across the stairs. But he unlocked it and took us down the long narrow hallway to the 'ghost room.' It was absolutely wonderful! By flashlight, in the dark, it was even better! Room 24, where the ghost had been seen!

"Luke slept on the third floor, when the weather was decent, and we asked him, 'Aren't you afraid to sleep up here?' Oh yeah he was! He was very much afraid to sleep up there, and yes, he had seen things and had heard things, regularly, but he hadn't searched them out in the night! He would just cover up his head and go to sleep.

"Well, anyway, we went back to our room to go to bed, and suddenly I became very ill. Now this is the truth, I swear! I hadn't eaten anything out of the ordinary. Just what the rest of the family ate that night. I'm not a person who is taken to illness. I rarely see a doctor. It came on so suddenly, right after we had been upstairs on the third floor. Minute by minute I was getting worse. It seemed to progress so quickly! It was sort of like the flu, but not like any flu I could remember ever having. I wasn't in any pain, but I was like fainting and at one point, vomiting. It wasn't like any kind of food poisoning or indigestion, and I felt really strange. John went down the hall to see if the kids were all right, and they were fine. And as the illness got worse and worse, I became really frightened. John and I discussed trying to get a pilot to get me to Juneau, for Skagway doesn't have a doctor. The road was closed and the ferry had left. The weather wasn't the greatest and flying out in a small plane in the middle of the night would be rather dangerous. So, I thought I would hold off for a while to see if this thing would pass.

"There are two beautifully carved beds in room 14. Placed so that the ends of the beds are at the door. I laid down on one of the beds. If we saw a ghost, we had a video camera loaded and ready to go at the foot of the bed, as well as a Minolta X-700 with high speed surveillance film and a Vivitar with a flash. I said to John, 'I'm getting worse,' for I was at the point where I kept passing out and coming to, and I was really scared. Finally, at some point, I just slept.

"Approximately two hours went by. When I opened my eyes, I was lying facing the door with my back to the window. My husband was lying on his back with his arm under my neck. When I opened my eyes, I was looking at the door and my eyes felt kind of fuzzy — sort of out of focus. At least I thought that's what it was! John whispered to me, 'What are you looking at?' and I said, 'I don't know. What *is* that?' and he answered back, 'I don't know either, but I've been watching it for two hours!'

"I mean, that's quite a statement from a skeptic! He saw what I saw, so it wasn't my eyes! We just lay there, trying to put things in proper perspective, trying to describe to each other what we were looking at, and figured it was a light form of some sort. At least to me, that was the best description. It had substance, but we could see through it. It was large. It went clear to the top of the door. It had human form, but I couldn't tell if it was a man or a woman. It was just a pulsating sort of light form. It almost covered the door, and we watched it for another hour and just whispered to each other.

"I was so fascinated, I had almost forgotten how awful I felt! We didn't get off the bed, and we were so mesmerized that we forgot to use the cameras! Quite frankly, it didn't even enter our minds to take a picture of this 'thing!' It moved, but it didn't move from the door. So there was *no way* we were going to leave the room. We thought about switching on the light, but the switch was near the door, and we

11

certainly didn't want to move near this thing to put out the lights! And here was John, who scoffed at these things, too spellbound to make an attempt either.

"Finally, it started to move from the door. And as it disappeared, I immediately felt well again! As soon as this thing was gone, I got better! Now, don't tell me that this was the flu. It doesn't work that way. Immediately we jumped up and opened the drapes — no street lights. We went out into the hall. We did just about everything we could think of to recreate what had happened in the room. But we couldn't do it. We couldn't bring anything into that room — lights, shadows, anything that might recreate what we had seen. Finally, we went to bed and slept, totally exhausted, and woke up in the morning feeling great. You know, if I had been ill from something that a medical doctor could put a finger on, I would have still been sick. Or at least have some sort of 'hangover' from it all. But I was just fine. No lingering effects at all. It was the strangest thing.

"We packed and boarded the ferry Saturday and headed home to Juneau. We all agreed that we loved Skagway and wanted to make it our new home. So, after landing in Juneau we started making arrangements to move.

"I'm a licensed hairdresser, and in the shop several days later I was telling some of my clients about our experience with the ghost, or whatever it was. Two young men came in to have their hair cut. While cutting one young man's hair, I was telling him about our trip to Skagway and our future move. He said that he and his friend had backpacked all over Alaska during the previous summer, and they had stayed in the Golden North. I asked him if he had seen the ghost, and he said he didn't know there was a ghost. So I told him of my experience with the light form and my illness, and he said, 'Wait a minute. Stop cutting my hair,' and turned to his friend and said, 'Are you listening to this — this is spooky — this is really weird.' He had the same thing happen to him. Not the light form at the door, but the same episode of illness. Exactly as it happened to me. He had been so suddenly sick that he had to get the paramedic out of bed in the middle of the night. He said that he hadn't been sick for years and had not been sick since. I asked him what room he had stayed in, and he said he guessed that it had been Room 9.

"After we moved to Skagway, I leased a space over a gift shop for my hairdressing business. One day I was leaning down over the balcony, and this young couple came in the shop below and started talking to the manager about the frightening experience they had just had at the Golden North in Room 24. That a light form or something appeared and scared them so badly that they moved out in the middle of the night.

"But to get back to Mary — I think she is just some sort of a legend. Whether she ever existed, I don't know. But strange things go on in that hotel!"

I'm sure that what John and Sharon Garland saw was *not* Mary!

A young Skagway man who asked me not to use his

name was also frightened in the hotel. He had lived in Skagway most of his life. Consequently he had heard many things about the ghosts in the Golden North Hotel. One night, he and one of his friends decided that they would stay in Room 24 in the hotel, just to see what might happen.

He said that he woke up in the middle of the night and something was pressing on his chest and choking him at the same time. it took him a while to get rid of whatever was doing this, because he could hardly move or cry out for help. When he was finally able to talk, he convinced his friend, in no uncertain terms, that home in bed would be a much safer place!

They say buildings hold memories and events for sometimes hundreds of years. This historic old hotel had once been a warehouse and an Army barracks. Could someone have been murdered in this place before it was moved and became a hotel? Certainly some of the "vibes" were pretty hard to handle. Skagway, in the early years during the gold rush, had been a pretty violent place.

Whether Mary was a legend or not, we will never really know. But then again, we might!

It seems to me that this hotel certainly needed a seance! Besides, what's a good ghost story without throwing in a well-conducted, "hold-hands-around-the-table" demonstration?

So, move over Mary, enter "Laura Vandermeer," the restless soul in room 21.

On March 30, 1975, three ladies named Bobbie, Dee and Kay got together in the hotel to hold a seance.

As Dee tells the story in a paper she wrote, "Our ghost-chasing credentials were none too impressive. Both Kay and I were very psychic, but our talents lay in other directions. However, Bobbie had done some spiritual exorcism work with a group in Reno at one time, and on the strength of this we decided to see what we could do at the Golden North Hotel."

The hotel was not yet open for the tourist season. Occasionally they had a guest, but not like the summer crowds. So the three of them made arrangements with the caretaker to hold a seance at night in Room 21. Following behind the caretaker, three rather apprehensive ladies climbed the stairs to the third floor that night, and then the caretaker made a fast exit. They were left alone with whatever was in that room.

Dee went on to say, "When we entered Room 21, each one of us had a definite, yet different, feeling that some presence other than ourselves was there. Kay felt an icy chill, and every hair on Bobbie's body stood up! There was no doubt in our minds that there was something unusual in the room."

Here I would like to say that it has been proven by a number of serious research people in the field of parapsychology, that when there is a phenomena of some kind in a room, the temperature drops. Usually in the exact spot where this presence makes itself known.

The women arranged three chairs in a circle and placed a candle on the floor for concentration. They began to meditate to clear their minds and see if they could make contact with the presence in the room.

"Within a short period of time I had a mental impression of a woman standing in the doorway," Dee wrote. "She was small, about five foot-four inches and thin. About one hundred fifteen pounds. Her face was pinched and her complexion sallow. She seemed to be in her mid-twenties. Her hair was a 'mousy' shade of brown, piled high on her head with a tendril falling over one shoulder. She stood in the doorway wringing her hands as if afraid to come into the room. She was dressed in a light blue dressing gown, ornamented with small appliqued flowers that looked like pansies. I tried to speak to her telepathically, to ease her fears and convince her to come into the room with us. After unsuccessfully attempting this for a while, I broke my concentration, and with it, the contact I had made with the ghost."

Dee continued, "Bobbie and Kay broke their concentration at the same time and we compared notes. Kay had seen nothing, but Bobbie described exactly what I had seen!"

They then decided that perhaps this young woman needed a "medium" to speak through and agreed that, when it happened, they would direct the spirit to Bobbie, for she was more experienced in this sort of thing.

Again the three women relaxed and concentrated on trying to reach the ghost. And Dee described the following:

"Almost immediately my mental impression was

that the ghost was still standing in the doorway watching us apprehensively. Again I repeated over and over a mental message not to be afraid. That we were there to help her. Bobbie and Kay had linked hands and almost immediately Bobbie's body became almost rigid. Her hands flew apart from Kay's, and Bobbie's face changed slightly. It became drawn and pulled back from her normal expression. And in a voice not wholly her's, the spirit's story came tumbling out.

"Bobbie's hands reached up and held the sides of her head, and a voice cried, *'The wind. Oh the wind is driving me crazy! I'm so afraid, so terribly afraid. I'm afraid of everything. I'm afraid of you. I'm frightened all the time!'*

"Bobbie dropped her hands into her lap and started wringing them together again and the voice went on, *'And I am so cold, so very cold all the time. Why oh why must I be so cold and afraid and why does the wind howl so?'*"

Dee said it was obvious that Bobbie couldn't say anything back to this young woman, and Kay was in no position to break her concentration to speak. So Dee was the likely candidate for the job.

Taking courage into her hands, Dee verbally reassured the young woman that they were there to help her and that she was not to fear any of them. The voice said, *"I'm grateful, so very grateful you came. I've been waiting so long. I've been worried and afraid."*

Dee's first question was the obvious, asking the young woman her name.

The ghost answered, *"Laura Ann. Although my father used to call me Annie Laurie and used to sing the song to*

17

me."

"What is your last name, Laura Ann?"

"My name is Vandermeer."

Dee asked, "Laura, why are you here?"

"Richard told me to stay in the room until he got back. He told me that there were obnoxious men in the lobby and on the street, and I was only safe if I stayed in the room."

"Hasn't Richard ever come back?"

"No. He said that he would be gone a little while, but he hasn't returned yet. He's been gone for such a long time and I've been so lonely and worried."

"Do you think that something could have happened to him? There is a possibility that something happened to him and he passed away and can't come back to you," Dee suggested.

"Richard told me to stay in the room until he got back and that's what I'm going to do," the young woman flatly stated.

"Why did you come to Skagway?" Dee asked.

"Richard came to get rich and he wanted to marry me. So, I came up here to get married to him. I love him very much."

Again Dee said, "Laura, what happened to you in this room? Did somebody hurt you, or were you sick or something?"

After she thought a while, Laura answered, *"After Richard left I did get sick. I remember being very hot and then very cold and my chest hurt. I had trouble breathing. Then very suddenly I was fine. No more pain or trouble. I didn't even cough anymore. I was just cold all the time."*

Dee was in a quandary as to how to tell this gentle

soul that her physical body no longer existed, and she tried to explain the best she could.

"*I don't believe you! How could I be dead?*" she snapped. *"I'm talking to you right now!"*

Dee went on to explain that Laura was using Bobbie's physical body to speak to all of them. She looked at Bobbie's face, and it seemed to be relaxed in deep thought. Then Laura's voice came tumbling out, *"Oh my goodness! What am I to do? What am I to do now?"*

Dee said that Bobbie's body was reacting to the emotion, and she was almost crying. So she tried the best she knew to explain to the spirit that they would help her find Richard.

Laura's voice, through Bobbie, asked in a fearful way, *"But how am I going to do that? How do I know where I'm going?"*

Dee thought about this for a while, for she honestly had no more idea how a soul left this plane of existence and went on to the other than Laura did. But she did know that usually the process was almost automatic. So perhaps the use of concentration and imagination on the part of the three of them just might do it.

So Dee said to the spirit, "We'll help you Laura. Just concentrate on going to your Richard and we'll help you get to the right place."

Using all the concentration Kay and she could muster, they imagined the ceiling in the room opening up and clouds appearing, and a hand extending down through the clouds. At the same time, they concentrated on seeing Laura rise from Bobbie's inert figure on the chair, and extending her hand to meet the hand that they assumed would be Richard's. Just before Laura's figure disappeared into the clouds, Dee said that Laura looked back and smiled. That her smile was one of gratitude, relief and joy. And then she was gone.

After a short period of rest, the three women proceeded through prayer to seal the room, so that no vacuum existed that could trap another spirit in this room. Then they left.

As Dee related later, "Was this a true experience or was it the working of the overactive imagination of three impressionable ladies? Our intention was not to prove anything to anyone, just to rid the hotel of an unwanted guest."

Going back to the history of the hotel, Laura Ann Vandermeer must have had the same experience as Mary had, in transferring her spirit from one place to the other. The Golden North, as it is now, did not exist when either of these spirits supposedly had died in their respective rooms, 21 and 24.

I looked through the death records at Skagway City Hall and came up with nothing. But please bear in mind that recording things in those days was rather a "hit and miss" proposition. I also searched the beautiful Gold Rush Cemetery at the end of town and found no marker with the name Laura Ann Vandermeer. There is a "Mary" on a marker there, but no one was ever able to slow Mary's spirit down long enough to get her last name!

The seance was held in March of 1975, and the three ladies felt that they had dispatched a troubled spirit on to a better place. However, John and Sharon Garland might argue this point. Was what they saw Mary or Laura? I have a feeling that it wasn't. As Sharon said, there are things out there that are both troubled and evil, and we have to guard ourselves against them.

Just because a physical body dies, does not mean that the problems it has dies with it, or that the evil personality goes with the body. It may choose to stay here.

It is said that energy and matter can not be destroyed, only transformed. *We* are energy and *we* are forever!

Hey, Soapy Smith, are you still out there?

2

"Delilah" — C. Caldwell

SKAGWAY, ALASKA

"Delilah"

The Notorious
Ghost of the
Red Onion Saloon

On the corner of Second and Broadway stands a rather picturesque old saloon named the Red Onion, owned and operated by Jan Wrentmore. When the tourists land in Skagway by cruise ship in the summer months, Jan greets them at the dock, dressed in period costume, and introduces herself as "Madame Jan," inviting them to come and enjoy themselves at her saloon.

Back in the early 1900s, the Red Onion was one of Skagway's most notorious "houses of pleasure" and was then located near the outskirts of town on the corner of Sixth and State streets, one block over from the "red light district."

Many of the old landmark buildings in Skagway were moved to different locations during the reorganization of the city (circa 1908) into the way it looks today. Most of the buildings were on "skids" and relatively easy to move.

Walking into the Red Onion today, one can very easily leave present reality, for the building is almost exactly as it was during the time of the gold rush. Occasionally someone will sit down at the old upright piano and play "honky-tonk" music of days gone by, but today the Red Onion resounds with more modern music, thanks to visiting musicians off the cruise ships. Whatever the Red Onion was from 1898 to the early 1900s, it is now one of the happiest and most lively bars in town.

However, after all the customers have gone and the bar is closed, eerie things happen. Someone else guards the Red Onion with an animosity that has scared quite a number of people.

Jan and I talked over a cup of coffee at the Sweet Tooth Cafe one afternoon:

JAN: I personally have a very special feeling when I go in the building. I feel really safe. Really at home there and protected. I have the confidence that nothing very bad would happen to me while I'm in there, even late at night. But it's mainly the men who work for me, who are there when I'm not, that have reported various incidents — the janitors and people that look after the building.

SHIRLEY: What have they told you?

JAN: Basically, they've reported a hostile female presence. And a couple of them reported that something stopped them when they were going up the stairs. That's where the bordello used to be, the second floor. The main thing was that if they went upstairs to check on where the bordello used to be, they felt that they were being scrutinized and watched

26

to make sure they didn't do any damage. There have been times when I have been out of town, and no one was there, the plants got watered and my office door was open. No one else watered the plants, I was told, and I kept the office door locked. No one else has the key. I feel that it is a woman who doesn't like men.

One time my bartender and my handyman were working downstairs. The bartender had come in the front door. It was about eleven in the morning. The handyman had heard noises upstairs and he thought the bartender was up there, until he saw her walk in the front door! And he said, "What are you coming in that door for, I thought you were upstairs — I heard noises up there!" She said, "I haven't been upstairs!" They looked at each other and listened to the footsteps, the pounding and the feet running! So, they called the police. The police arrived. There were two of them and they went up the back stairs. There's no way out of the upstairs. Anyone coming down from there, or going up, would have to pass the people on the main floor. There's a door up there but it's always locked because there's no stairway down from the outside any more. If anyone ever opened that door and tried to leave by that door, it would be an awful drop to the ground below! The police went up the stairs with their guns drawn and searched the whole place and never found anything.

SHIRLEY: When did this happen?

JAN: The spring of 1983. As I said, the door leading out of the second floor is always locked. No one has the key and it's a heavy lock. If anyone had

27

tried to open that door, they would have had to break it down, and then they wouldn't have been able to close it. The janitor that worked for me has since died, but he would tell me that he would be working and suddenly feel cold air in places, and then he would smell women's perfume. This was early in the morning. And he'd just stop and hunt everywhere to see where it was coming from and find nothing. And days later he would be working again and he'd hit a real strange cold spot in a different part of the bar, and he'd smell that perfume again.

In a way, I'm glad that some time later the Fire Marshal came in and had me close the upstairs for tours because he felt it was a fire hazard. So, I took all my antiques out of there to a place called "Liarsville." It's a place I've set up out on the river like a gold camp, exactly as it was in 1898. The fellow that I hired to look after the place — keep an eye on things — to live out there, was a biker from Juneau. A big, tough guy who wore all the leather. And one day he told me there was a ghost out there! I never mentioned anything about the Red Onion ghost. Anyway, he came to me one day and said, "You know, I sense a very hostile presence of a female out there." He used the very same words that the handyman had used at the Red Onion! This female presence must have followed the old clothing and the antiques from the Red Onion out to Liarsville, to keep an eye on them. You know, I never put the idea in this man's head. And if you knew him, you'd never believe that he would admit to seeing a ghost. And for that matter, even believing in ghosts. I think after a while he became quite comfortable with her. And he claimed that she would wake him up if he overslept in the morning. That he could see her shadow against the tent wall and she would bang on the canvas to get him awake. If she was hostile towards men, he must have been an exception. Maybe she sensed that he was the fine man that he really is!

In a column written after the gold rush, the famous northern newspaper wit, Stroller White, related a story about finding a man on the ground in the alley next to the Red Onion Saloon. The man, who had accompanied the Stroller on a ship north to Skagway in the spring of 1898, was weeping. He said that a girl named Delilah broke his heart, took all of his money, and kicked him out. Stroller said he took the man in and let him sleep all night under his printing press at the *Skaguay News.* On the following morning, the Stroller helped the fellow secure a job on a ship, shoveling coal in exchange for passage south.

No one has ever actually seen Delilah, but she's still at the Red Onion and Liarsville, making her presence known late at night. And if necessary, she even haunts the daylight hours.

As Jan says, "I don't mind really. After all, she does water my plants!"

3

31

The district recorder's office, pictured above in May, 1900, was later expanded into the house on the right.

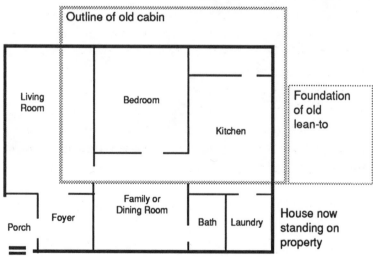

Outline of old cabin

| Living Room | Bedroom | Kitchen | Foundation of old lean-to |

Family or Dining Room

Porch | Foyer | Bath | Laundry

House now standing on property

32

"Haunted Rocking Chair"

The Old District
Recorder's Cabin

In January of 1989, Kevin and Leah Nicholas lived in Skagway near the corner of Sixth and Alaska Streets. Kevin was a teacher of science and physical education at the Skagway Public School, and Leah worked as a secretary for the National Park Service. They were both in their late twenties: bright, level-headed people who were not overly imaginative in any way. Certainly, when I spoke with them, they seemed to have used their minds in a rational way to explain what had happened in their home.

Leah called me one day and explained that they had been having some strange things happen in their house which they could not explain, and would I come over and talk with them. We were seated in their warm and gracious dining room:

SHIRLEY: When did you first move into this house?

KEVIN: Halloween, a year ago, October, 1987.

33

SHIRLEY: Do you know who lived here before you did?

KEVIN: It has been a rental for summer people. After Bill Bailey bought it, the (White Pass) railroad shut down and he left. Since that time quite a number of people have moved in and out. Mostly summer people.

LEAH: Bill Bailey now lives in College, Alaska, up near Fairbanks. He's working on the (Alaska) railroad up there. There were a lot of things left in the house that belonged to Bill and his ex-wife that were stored here. So it took us about three weeks to pack a lot of those things before we actually moved in, and I spent a lot of time over here by myself. And there were periods of time when I would be here alone and didn't think I was by myself. It felt like someone was with me. I'd be back in the rear of the house doing laundry, and there would be a commotion of some sort, and I would come out to see what was going on, and there'd be no one out here. I thought, "Well, I'm just hearing things." And after we moved in permanently, I was doing dishes one night when Kevin was away on a trip, and I had a feeling that, *wow*, someone was right behind me!

SHIRLEY: Did you feel any change of temperature?

LEAH: Well, my shoulders. I just had a chill right here on my shoulders, and you know how you just get that pressure right here on the back of your neck? It's like someone has their hands on you!

KEVIN: Like someone has invaded your space.

LEAH: I've had that happen to me here in this house two or three different times. I stood there at the sink and I didn't *dare* look in the mirror in front of me. I just *knew* that there was someone behind me. I just shut my eyes and said (in my mind), "Go away!"

SHIRLEY: Were you afraid?

LEAH: I just didn't want to see whatever it was behind me. I don't know!

SHIRLEY: When did all of this first start?

LEAH: The minute I started moving things into this house. The house hadn't been vacant that long. They'd had some summer people in here.

KEVIN: We started moving some of our things in here and started moving some of Bailey's things out. That was the first of October, 1987.

LEAH: And that's when we started hearing that rocking chair sound.

SHIRLEY: Well, first of all, let me ask you, has anything like this ever happened to you before? I'm thinking that it might be something that you brought with you.

KEVIN: We never have before.

LEAH: I've never had those types of feelings before either.

SHIRLEY: Well, how did you know what it was then?

LEAH: Common sense. I didn't start thinking that we had something like a ghost until after I started checking out what this creaking was in the bedroom. We finally determined that it couldn't be loose boards, loose wires — the paneling wasn't loose. It didn't creak when you walked on the floor. I'd go over and shake the door and then slam it, thinking it might be the door. No wind. It would creak in the middle of the day and it would creak at night.

SHIRLEY: For how long a time?

KEVIN: It would creak for about an hour and then it would stop.

LEAH: This is what's funny. It would creak its way up the wall to the ceiling and then creak its way down again.

KEVIN: It was like, in the very corner of the bedroom. I even crawled under the house to check out the foundation in that corner, and it wasn't in the foundation. I stayed under the house and listened to it stop and then start creaking again. Sometimes it would stay at the floor level and creak, and then up the wall it would go again and stay for a while near the ceiling, before it came down again. That's the only place in the house that it would do this. And it would do it when people were around (not just for us alone), but other people could hear it too. We would tell them, "Hey, it's creaking again — why don't you come in and hear it." That's when they said, "That's *not* natural."

SHIRLEY: Well, tell me about the television set. The one that you mentioned to me earlier?

LEAH: That's when Kevin and his parents had come to visit us. That was this past summer and Kevin and his father had gone to Hoonah, hunting, and we women were here at the house, meaning Kevin's mother and my mother. My mother was sleeping out here on the sofa and Kevin's mother was sleeping with me in the bedroom on the waterbed. We had been away for several days to Juneau and had come back that night, tired, and we kinda hit the hay early. Mom had gone around and turned all the lights out. We'd been in bed for a while and we had gotten to talk about the ghost, and Carol (my mother-in-law) said, "I know he's here. I feel a presence." Let me say this, before I had told her anything at all, she had an experience the first night when she was sleeping in the living room on the hide-a-bed. She had a bad time trying to sleep. She said something had been pressing her feet into the mattress all night long, and she could hardly move her feet. It was then we told her some of the things that had happened to us in the house. So, that night (after we came back from Juneau), we were just laying there and talking again about the ghost, and I said to her, "By the way.... Oh my gosh, look at the TV!" It had a real faint glow. I called out to the living room and said, "Mother, come in here!" So she got up and came into the bedroom. I said, "Look at the TV!" And it was really glowing by that time — not a bright glow — but it was glowing.

SHIRLEY: Was it plugged in?

LEAH: No, because we had been in Juneau. Kevin had always told me to unplug electrical things before I took a trip, and I had gone around and made sure these things were not plugged in. By that time it had gotten mother really scared. So, she jumped into bed with us, and by the time we had done our chuckling and giggling about the TV glowing, it started to go away. I finally got out of bed to check the TV and see if I had forgotten about unplugging it before we left on the trip, and it was still unplugged. It seemed that the minute we had started talking about the ghost, it sort of turned on all by itself and started to glow. When we finally realized that this was something strange and stopped joking about it, the glow just faded away. Like he's trying to communicate or something through the TV, and he didn't like anyone making fun of him.

SHIRLEY: You said something to me earlier about the fact that "he" moved things around the house.

LEAH: Kevin loves to rearrange the furniture, and he was always changing pictures from one wall to the other (points to the ones in the living room). These pictures in the corner of the living room would always be crooked. We'd go over and straighten them, and in an hour or two, they'd be crooked again. Now, if we put them on another wall like this one (points to the outside wall on the south side of the house), they wouldn't be moved. It just seemed that he didn't like anything on the walls on the other side of the house, either in the far corner of the living room or the far corner of our bedroom.

SHIRLEY: What about the moving of the furniture?

KEVIN: Leah's mom says she thinks he doesn't like the furniture moved. While she was here, we moved a few things around in the living room. That night she was up all night because something kept shaking her shoulders, like someone does when they want you to wake up.

LEAH: Those funny vibrations I was telling you about? Well, it felt like he had his hands right here on your chest and he would just shake you until you woke up, and there was no one there!

SHIRLEY: Anything else happen to your mother while she was here?

KEVIN: Oh yes. She saw what she described like a sheer curtain blowing across her bed from the front of the house — right there in that corner. She thought for a while that it might have been a light from a passing car. But no cars had passed, and there are no street lights at this end of the street. So what she was seeing was a "ghost curtain" in a "ghost window!" She tried to go back to sleep and she could hear this "swishing" sound. So she forced her eyes open and saw this curtain again, like a light cloud of grey moving through the air.

(We looked later at the living room corner and determined that the previous building that had been on this property had had a window on that spot. In the picture of the cabin, it had a sheer curtain on that window. The new house, on the old foundations, didn't have a window in that spot)

SHIRLEY: Did it actually look like a curtain or could it have been what some people call ectoplasm?

KEVIN: She said it looked like a sheer curtain. And she also said she "knew" that we had a ghost in our rocking chair.

SHIRLEY: Oh, you have a ghost in your rocking chair?

KEVIN: That's what we call the creaking in the

wall. We call it our rocking chair because it creaks just like an old rocking chair.

LEAH: On the night of the Fourth of July, Kevin and I had gone to bed and I started having those strange vibration feelings, and this time it was really *hard*. So, I came flying out of bed and said to Kevin, "Wake up, we're having another earthquake!" And my thoughts were to get to my mother so she wouldn't be frightened. So I went charging into the living room and said, "Mother, Mother, are you all right?" And she said, "Leah, what's wrong?" And I said to her that I thought we were having another earthquake, but that it probably was just "him" again. That night also, she had seen the curtains flying across her bed again.

SHIRLEY: You know, I have something written down in my notebook that happened to someone that stayed at the Skagway Inn, and I have a feeling that this might give you some idea as to the mystery that's going on in this house. It says, "In this old building, which is actually several buildings, the 'psychic' location of rooms and walls isn't limited to modern boundaries. A piece of the old building might include the 'psychic yard' or alleyway of the ghostly structure. In other words, the ghostly realm 'slides' across ordinary reality." Of course, this was how someone felt about the Skagway Inn. But it could also relate to what's happening here.

LEAH: Oh, I understand! Actually "he" is in his own space of the old cabin.

KEVIN: Right! He actually is in his own house. He could go back and forth there, where there could have been a door. Maybe the cabin had a wall here back to his living quarters. And we are in *his* living quarters, and where our bed is located, is the door that was in *his* wall. And there could have been a rocking chair approximately where our closet is now!

LEAH: It has always been so strange that we have never had any actions in this part of the house. Just where his cabin was located.

SHIRLEY: Have you ever checked out the location of the foundations of the old cabin?

KEVIN: Yeah, come back here (We walked into the kitchen and looked out of the back window). See that slight rise back there? That's where the end of the foundation of the original house was. And that hollow spot, surrounded with stones, is where the old woodshed must have been.

LEAH: (Returning to the dining room) You know, even our cat acts strange sometimes. When she comes running through the house, she follows the wall, the new wall. And sometimes she acts like she is being chased by something. She won't go into any part of the house except the "new structure." Maybe our ghost didn't like cats, or the cat can feel or see something we can't?"

KEVIN: Have Leah tell you about the bubbles in our waterbed.

LEAH: Yes, Kevin said that he's never felt them. But sometimes it feels like it is boiling. You know, how you see a pan of hot water and you see those bubbles on the bottom? And they come to the top and start "popping." This was the sensation I was getting, but just on my side of the bed. Kevin never felt anything.

KEVIN: The only thing I felt, when she was telling me about this, was like a cat had jumped on the bed. But the cat wouldn't come into our bedroom.

LEAH: Well, it could have been "him" shaking the bed, so that it made these little bubbles. We keep our waterbed fairly warm. And I thought, this bed *couldn't* be boiling! But it felt like it was, in the sense that it felt like these little bubbles were coming up and popping. But I didn't *see* anything, I just had the sensation. I've never disbelieved, but I've never had anything happen to me that made me *truly* believe in ghosts, until this started happening here in this house!

I went to City Hall in Skagway and looked up the records and deeds concerning the house in which Kevin and Leah lived. From what I was able to determine, the cabin (see photo) was built in 1898. The lot was bought on February 3, 1898 for use as both a business and residence by a young man who was about twenty-one years old. His name was John V. Ostrander, and he was the District Recorder. On January 15, 1910, the property was bought by Phillip W. Snyder, and he tore down the log cabin and built a new house on the old foundations — at least the new house covered the old foundations. Mr. Snyder built several houses in the same area, including one across the street. Mr. Snyder was a bachelor and lived alone.

It was next to impossible for me to find out anything about the young man who built the old log cabin. Back in the early days, Skagway was a very transient community. It was a town wild with dirty politics, gambling, contagious diseases, gold fever and extreme change.

Did something violent happen to this young man, John Ostrander? He was only twenty-one when he built the cabin, and when it was bought by someone else, he would have been only thirty-three. Did he leave Skagway? Or did he become a victim of one of the many things that happened in Skagway during those violent times?

Or is this ghost someone else?

Whomever it is, someone has come back to claim the cabin and his favorite rocking chair.

Kevin and Leah Nicholas now live in Burden, Kansas, where life has been made a little more lively by the birth of their twin boys, Morgan and Zachary, on May 10, 1989.

4

"CHARLIE"

DEZADEASH, YUKON

"Charlie"

The Ghost Who
Hated Tour Buses

Heading west on the Alaska Highway from Whitehorse, Yukon about eighty miles, one comes to Haines Junction. Here the highway goes south to Haines, Alaska. Heading out on the Haines Highway about twenty-five miles, one sees beautiful Dezadeash Lake, which is about fifteen miles long.

Kho-klux, the great Chief of the Chilkat Indians, called it "Dasar-dee-Ash" or "Dasa-dee-Arsh," meaning "Lake of the Big Winds." After following this lake, which borders the highway for about ten miles, you come to Dezadeash Lodge on the right side of the highway.

Dezadeash Lodge "houses" one of the most humorous ghosts in all of the Yukon Territory. How long "he" has been there no one knows, but anyone who stays for the night or stops for dinner and drinks in the gracious dining room/bar should be cognizant of the fact that no matter who runs the lodge, "Charlie" really owns the place. And they had better have a sense of humor, or plan on eating or sleeping somewhere else down the road. Especially if they come on a tour bus!

In our living room one night in Whitehorse, Nancy Lavine, her friend Garth, my husband Bert, and myself talked about "Charlie" and his antics during the time Nancy and Garth ran the Dezadeash Lodge. The conversation (and laughter) went as follows:

SHIRLEY: When did you start experiencing problems in the lodge?

NANCY: Well, I guess when we had been there about two weeks.

SHIRLEY: What year was this?

NANCY: Starting in the early spring of 1985, through the summer and into the winter. Actually it started with an argument between Garth and I. He said to me, "Why are you looking so bedraggled," and I said, "I just need a bath," and he said, "Why don't you just take a bath then, just go do it. With the seventeen units there's got to be an empty bathtub somewhere!" And I said, "Yes, but not for me. I just can't get any hot water out of them!" Garth said, "Well that seems strange, 'cause I take a bath twice a day," and I said, "I know you do, but every time I go, there's no hot water!"

So this became an argument. "Well, there's something you're not doing right!" And I said, "Yes, but I don't know what it is!" And Garth would go and check it, and there was hot water. And I would go and there was *no* hot water. So I began to feel that I was totally incompetent!

And then there would be incidents like I couldn't open the fridge, and I would think there must be a vacuum here of some kind. It just feels so tight, I can't get it open. So Garth would come along and he would open it with no problem.

So anyway, again I'm thinking, I'm just overworked, overtired, too much to think about, and I don't know what's what anymore.

Then finally our chef came from Dawson City. He was an older fellow and gave you the feeling that there wasn't anything he hadn't experienced or didn't know about.

Well, we did all right for a while. And then we started getting the tour buses. And every time a tour bus would come in, the fridge wouldn't open. Our chef was a little man, and he would put his foot up against the wall, and he'd be pulling on the fridge door at the same time, and it just wouldn't open. Finally he said, "Lookit, you do know that there's a ghost here!"

He said that he had heard him in his room. He had worked in the lodge previously, prior to us taking over, and then he came back to work for us. So he was somewhat familiar with the place. And he said, "Lookit, we just have to make sure we don't put anything in the fridge when the tour bus is coming. We have to get water, 'cause there won't be water, and fill the containers, because somehow the spirit doesn't like tourists or tour buses!"

SHIRLEY: You mean you couldn't get any water at all?

49

NANCY: That's right!

SHIRLEY: How long did this go on?

NANCY: The whole time we were there. And not always the fridge. I mean it wouldn't always stick, only when the tour buses came in, then it gave us problems. Like if we were serving desserts, we had to get them all out on the counter, including the whipped cream. Then as soon as the first bus would come into the drive, off went the water (in the kitchen). And if we needed anything out of the fridge, forget it! Seems like he knew we were depending on using the fridge for the customers off the bus. He must have had a good ear for bus engines! We just had to keep one step ahead of him and have it all out on the counter!

SHIRLEY: So how did you handle this?

NANCY: Well, we learned to live with him. It really was rather humorous.

SHIRLEY: You say, "him." How do you know this?

NANCY: Well, I don't know if he was a "him" really, but that's what the cook said. That it was a "him." The fellow that we hired to run the bar, he didn't stay very long. He was quite disturbed by all of this, and he said that someone was always walking by the window, which was totally impossible. I'm talking about the little window in the kitchen door, between the bar and the kitchen. He said that someone was always walking by on the other side. There was a small light in the kitchen, but it didn't illuminate the kitchen enough for him to see anything but shadows. He was alone at night. He ran the bar at night. The kitchen was closed.

He was really bothered by this shadow walking back and forth, and he would go into the kitchen thinking that a customer had wandered back there by mistake. And there wasn't anyone back there. But he kept seeing this form go by the window and hearing footsteps. He finally quit.

We had a hard time keeping help unless they were a little open-minded about these things happening.

SHIRLEY: How old is Dezadeash Lodge?

NANCY: That's a good question, because it was built and then part of it was burned. But I think it was built in the Forties. About the time that they started building the Alaska Highway, during the war. It used to be called the Lakeside Lodge, because it's on Dezadeash Lake. And then at one time they called it Beloud Post. The motel units burned down and were rebuilt and some additions made. But the lodge itself basically goes back to the Forties.

SHIRLEY: Do you know if when the motel units burned down, if anyone died in the fire? Or has there ever been anyone who died there at any time during the history of the lodge? Do you know the history of this area?

NANCY: No, I don't. But it seems that the spirit has always been here. We call him "Charlie" for want of anything else to call him, especially in front of customers. When things got a little weird, or something strange happened, rather than say, "The ghost is at it again," we'd say, "Well, Charlie's acting up!" And the customers would think it was a staff member.

SHIRLEY: Did you ever talk to him?

NANCY: No, other than to say "smarten up" or "stop it" or "that's enough now!" And then he would usually stop. But as far as Garth and myself were concerned, we didn't feel threatened or anything. The things that he did were more mischievous than anything else. At least he finally allowed me to take a hot bath or shower when I wanted.

GARTH: Well, there are a couple of things that I can't quite explain. We had considerable trouble with the generator. Whether this has anything to do with Charlie is up to a person's own speculation, I suppose. The generator was an old machine. It had seen better days! And I was barely able to keep it going. As I recall there was one day when it had shut down. But there was something weird going on. The lights in the lodge were glowing. I use the word glow instead of just light, like it was down to one-quarter power. And I said to Nancy, "Well, it looks like the generator is bogging down again," like it was putting out seventy volts instead of one hundred ten. And I went out this time — it was getting dark — and the darn thing's not running at all! I'm not aware of this for sure. But with a machine down, why would the lights continue to glow? Now, there was just enough light to see down the hall. But with the machine down, how could this be? With a generator, it's either down or it's not! The generator's not hooked up to batteries or anything. It's a straight hookup. I'd get a little ticked off at the whole thing once in a while. But after a while the problem became humorous, and I had to laugh at it, 'cause it shut down a lot!

NANCY: I guess when we REALLY found out what was happening, like really believing, was when Garth came in one day from the garage and he was angry. We weren't busy and the staff and I were sitting around the long table in the kitchen. He came in all flustered and went running to the phone, picked it up and said, "Hello, hello!!" We all turned around and looked at him, and he turned and looked at us and said, "Can't somebody answer the phone?" And I said, "It didn't ring!" And Garth said, "It's been ringing and ringing!" I said, "Not in here!" "Well," he said, "It's ringing in the garage!"

I felt kind of bad, for we had a lull time and we were just sitting around, and he's out there working and having to take time to come in and answer the phone! I got up and said, "Look, if the phone was ringing, I'd answer it!"

So he went back out to the garage, and the phone kept ringing in the garage. Because of the close proximity of the generator, you can't hear anything even if you did answer the phone in the garage. So he would only be able to hear it faintly if he did answer it.

So we finally had NorthwestTel come out and check the whole thing out. They spent the whole day checking out the wires and everything and finally told us the phone in the garage wasn't working. As a matter of fact, it wasn't even hooked up! It had never rang then and it hasn't rung ever since!

GARTH: In November it starts to get really cold, and one of my jobs was to close up the motel units. I had to drain the pipes so they wouldn't freeze up. I would get the compressor unit, open all the taps and blow out all the lines. I had done all this and Nancy and I had gone into town. Mike stopped by and made himself at home, checked himself into one of the motel units, not knowing there wasn't any water. Mike was one of the fellows that helped us during the summer, and he would stop to visit us once in a while. Nancy and I came back from town, and there was Mike coming out of the shower room connected to the motel units. Now that part was all shut down for the winter. The bathrooms in the lodge itself were okay. And I said, after seeing him come out of that shower, "How are ya, Mike? What are you doin' coming out of *that* shower room?" And Mike said, "Oh, I was just havin' a shower." Nancy and I looked at each other and Nancy said, "Whatta you mean you were just having a shower? Couldn't have much water — Garth just shut all those units down." And Mike said, "Well, there was enough water. See, my towel's wet. My hair's wet. No problem with the water. It sure was cold in there though. But the water was nice and warm."

Now how he got enough water to take a shower, you got me! Mike has worked with us long enough to know that these things happen, and he just shrugged his shoulders and said, "Well, I guess Charlie just wanted me to have a shower!"

SHIRLEY: With all these things happening, is this the reason you finally quit running the lodge?

(laughter from both Nancy and Garth)

NANCY: Well, it was part of the reason. You just

had to have a sense of humor to keep up with the whole thing. It would irritate the staff. We couldn't keep staff. We had a bartender, like I told you, that finally quit. He just couldn't stand it any more. Between the spooky shadow that would go by the kitchen door at night, and whenever he took a shower, the shower head would fall off, or the water would run hot and cold and sometimes not at all, he left. He would try other rooms and could never get a hot shower. Same problem I had in the beginning, so he finally left.

Now the motel part seemed to be the most spooky part of the whole complex, as far as the rooms went. Once in a while there would be kind of resounding music that would come from above in the rooms. Yet when you went outside, you couldn't hear it. It would be "high class" music, you know, classical.

Now a survey crew were staying in the motel unit. There were six fellows that had three rooms. They complained about the music, but they said it really wasn't so loud as to be annoying, but it kept them awake at night. And one morning they said, "Would you ask whoever it is to shut off that music? We're not getting enough sleep." And I said, "But you're the only ones in the whole motel unit. I haven't rented a room out there for a week, except to you guys." They sort of looked at each other, and that was it. Well, that night they went from room to room looking for a radio. They were positive someone had left a radio on in one of the units somewhere. So, not having found anything, they said to me at breakfast, "Well, you know that you have some sort of ghost in there. You *do* realize that don't you?" So I just laughed and said, "Well, yes, we have been having some problems." And they told me, "That music has got to stop!" And from then on things got worse for them. I guess because they had complained. I told them that they would just have to accept it.

SHIRLEY: What was their attitude toward the possibility of the rooms being haunted? Did these men believe that sort of thing, or were they just kidding when they said a ghost was in there?

NANCY: I guess it kind of blew them away, because the last couple of weeks after that, they were all sleeping together in the same room. They were scared! Out where we were, they had no choice. We were the only place open for miles around. I suppose their only other choice was to sleep in the bush. I guess if they hadn't complained, Charlie, or whoever, would have eventually left them alone. There wasn't anything I could do about it really. I guess they could have told their employer, "Hey, there's a ghost in that motel. Can you arrange for a tent?" Now how would that have been accepted?

Later on that winter we started having the same problems with the rooms in the lodge, after the motel was closed for the season. There was one room in particular that we had trouble keeping rented. There was a bad storm that night and the highway to Haines was blocked. The pass was closed and we were booked solid with people. All the rooms were rented including Room 11. We rented that room to two men — two hardy, strong men. And they came back to the desk and said, "Would someone shovel the snow out, 'cause someone had left the door open and there was a snow drift in the room!" Now, my son was working with us that winter, and he said he would take care of it right away. He came back and said, "I don't know what's wrong with those guys. The door is shut and there's no snow in that room!" We didn't have any more complaints from them for about an hour, and again they came back and said they couldn't get into the bathroom. That the door was stuck. That there was a screw in it and it was screwed shut! So, again my son went out and checked the room. There was nothing wrong with it. The bathroom was fine. Not stuck — no screw in the door. The men checked out and said they were going to try and make it back to Haines Junction, back where they came from.

So, we thought we would try that room again. We were so full! This time two ladies checked into the room. They came back minutes later to tell us that they didn't have any lights! So, my son went out with some light bulbs. And by this time we *knew* who was doing it! Anyway, he went out with the new light bulbs. he told the ladies that he had changed the lights, but he hadn't, because the old ones were working just fine. That lasted for about two hours. The ladies came back and said there had been a bright flash, and all the lights went out. So my son went out there again with new light bulbs. But the ladies told us they had decided to go back to Haines Junction. They wouldn't say why, or anything, but we all knew why they were leaving! I guess the ladies' personalities had just conflicted with Charlie. That particular room had always given us problems. People would find all kinds of things wrong with it, and of course when we checked it out, there wasn't anything wrong.

SHIRLEY: Did you stop running the lodge because of all of this as well?

NANCY: Not really. There were a lot of things. For one, the traffic had slowed down through to Haines because of the Skagway road opening up. And more people were using that road to get through to the ferry.

GARTH: Let me say this. With Nancy, these things didn't seem to bother her. She seemed to be able to live with it and accept it a darn sight easier than I did! Her living patterns have been used to things that aren't always explainable. It just seems to be in her nature to accept these things. With my background, well, I just have to have an answer to explain these things. Like I have to have a logical explanation for all these things, it seems. Like Nancy says: "total logic!" We have had some pretty lively discussions over all of this. To me, there has *got* to be a reason. But where all of this was concerned, there just wasn't and I had to learn to accept that.

SHIRLEY: Have you ever had any experience with ghosts before or anything paranomal?

GARTH: No, to me this was a very special experience. These things were completely unexplainable. And as much as I tried to track it down, it just wasn't possible. So, if someone else after us wants to run the lodge, I would have to say that if they want it to be successful with all these things happening, they will have to be pretty flexible!

SHIRLEY: Since you left, has anyone else tried to run the place?

GARTH: Yes, some people from Haines. Very logical, sensible business people. I don't know what happened to the deal. Whether they had any problems with the bank or what, but I do know that the son of one of these men, an adult, spent three nights in the lodge. He was staying there supposedly just to clean up and get it ready. The neighbors out there told us that all the son said to them was that he would never spend another night in the place as long as he lived! Not long after that, the two men from Haines decided against the deal.

In the "winding up" of the lodge, after our lease was up, we were just doing the caretaking. I was dealing with one of the fellows at the bank. They were trying to sell the lodge, and apparently they had gone through a number of foreclosures with the place, and he was pretty frustrated. Here was a very logical individual, very meticulous, and he said to me, "are you sure there isn't some sort of a ghost out there in that place?" I found that to be rather unusual coming from him! But he brought it up himself for some particular reason. I found that to be rather strange, for it was totally out of character for him.

NANCY: There were several other incidents that happened at the lodge before we left. And this was in the bar itself. One of the (Kluane) park wardens came in one night. It was kind of lonely out there sometimes and we showed movies on the VCR. He came to find out when the movie was going to be on. I said, "As soon as we get the problems worked out with the generator, so just hang around," that we were definitely going to have a movie that night. The lights were flickering and he asked what the problem was. I said, "Oh, it's just Charlie again." I was trying to joke a bit. Now the park warden lives by himself out on the trail, and he has to walk home in the dark. Anyway, about this time all the glasses on the bar sort of flopped over on their sides, like dominos. And the warden said, "Was that an earth tremor?" And I said, no that it was just Charlie up to his old tricks again. Anyway, he didn't even finish his beer and he was *gone*! He never came back for the movie. Anyway, a few days later he came back and said, "Haven't you fixed those glasses yet?" And I told him that I couldn't, that it was like trying to balance an egg on one end, and there was nothing I could do. About this time, the lights in the bar went totally out. Up until then they were just flickering. When the lights came on again, then I knew I could straighten the glasses, and I did. It was just that simple, you know. If you just lived with it, there were no problems. But if you tried to fight it, forget it! You just had to have a sense of humor and work around the problem. It wasn't so bad for the local people, for they came to understand in their own way. But it wasn't good to try and run a business under those circumstances.

SHIRLEY: Do people around here know that there

is a ghost in the lodge?

NANCY: I kind of think so, because just before we went there, like six months before we took over, a rock had blown out of the fireplace. This rock just blew right out, and the place was full of people and it never hit anybody. I guess it scared everybody, but it never touched them. Theoretically, it never should have happened. It should have hit somebody, but it didn't. And one of the local men there said, "All right, Charlie, that's enough!" They said they picked up the rock and it was *cold*. So, it wasn't from the heat. All the other rocks in the face of the fireplace were *warm*.

Now before we leased the lodge to run it, we heard that the Natives from the Kluane Park area were offered a deal to buy it for the cost of fixing it up. The Natives of the community could take the lodge over with the help of the federal government. And they (the Natives) wouldn't touch it with a ten-foot pole! After our stay here, I thought, "Ah-ha, now I know *why*!"

Perhaps before the lodge was built, maybe someone died here. Maybe he had a cabin on the property, and now that the lodge is built here, he feels that he has a right to live in the lodge. Whoever it was, I'm sure, really enjoyed classical music. I remember hearing it at three in the morning in the kitchen. And later, Bonnie, the girl that worked for us at the time, finally said to me, "Do you hear music?" and I said, "Oh yes." And she said, "Do you think we could shut it off now?" I smiled and said, "I guess you'll have to ask Charlie."

Several months later, my husband and I drove to this beautiful lodge on Dezadeash Lake. It was closed. I walked up the drive and tried to peer in through the spaces in between the boards on the windows, and whispered: "Are you in there, Charlie?"

5

LAKE LABERGE, YUKON

"Ghost Ships"

The Phantom
Stern-wheelers

Many strange stories have been told about the Yukon lakes and rivers. One of the most famous is Robert Service's "Cremation of Sam McGee," which (as the story goes) took place on Lake Laberge. This vast lake, in the southcentral region of the Yukon, was part of the immense waterway system through to Dawson City during the days of the stern-wheelers.

So many of these magnificent ships ran aground and were wrecked on the sand bars, or sank trying to make it through the lake to the continuation of the Yukon River. Is it any wonder that some weird and strange "vibrations" remain, perhaps hovering over the lake and occasionally making themselves known?

According to historical records, there were three stern-wheelers that "came to rest" on the bottom of Lake Laberge. One was the steamer *A.J. Goddard*. She was built in San Francisco and re-assembled at Lake Bennett in June of 1899. She ran aground at a place that was later named Goddard's Point on Lake Laberge. Another boat that sank was the *Thistle*, which went down in a wind storm. The third ship that finished her career in Lake Laberge was built in St. Michael, Alaska in 1898 and was the first steamer into Dawson City from the lower Yukon River, arriving on June 8, 1898 during the height of the gold rush. She was originally named the *May West* and was sold to the Royal Northwest Mounted Police. They used her to patrol the Yukon and to assist many of the stampeders on their way to the Klondike gold fields. The *May West* was later renamed the *Vidette*, and she sank in the lower end of Lake Laberge in 1917.

Stern-wheelers on the Yukon River never had an easy passage. The current is swift (five to six miles per hour), shallow in places and marred with all kinds of narrow channels, shifting sand bars and rapids.

Other ships made it through the lake, only to be wrecked at places such as Five Finger Rapids and Rink Rapids. Perhaps the sightings of phantom ships on Lake Laberge are not necessarily ships that actually sank in the lake, but apparitions of others still heading for the gold fields.

According to the stories I have been told, there appear to be two phantom stern-wheelers that occasionally show themselves on the lake.

One steamer has been sighted a number of times sailing up the lake toward the Yukon River. The large stern wheel is turning but does not cause a large wave astern, as a normal wheel does. Instead it leaves a phosphorescent glow after it has gone by. As it approaches the head of the lake, it appears to "lift" over the sand bars which would have proved to be certain disaster for steamers in the old days.

According to people who have seen this phenomenon, there seems to be a name on the pilot house, but this ghost ship usually appears at dusk, and no one has yet been able to make out the name. Some have said that they could see a group of passengers standing on the upper deck.

Buzz and Josephine Sampson, who live in a lovely secluded cabin on the west shore of Lake Laberge, related to me the sighting of yet another phantom ship:

"This was in the summer of 1981," Josephine recalled, "and we had a couple visiting us from Edmonton, Alberta — Roy and Elaine Kramer, who came every year. And Josey and Paul had a fifth-wheel trailer here too. There were six of us altogether.

"I was the first one who noticed it. I went past Buzz, who was standing on the porch, and walked out to the lake and there it was! I said to Buzz, 'Oh look, at the ghost ship!' And everyone came running. We all stood there and watched it for two minutes. Buzz looked at it and said, "My God!' And Roy ran back into the cabin and got the glasses. Now Roy is a *real* skeptic. He looked through the glasses at the ship for people, for Buzz had asked him to see if he could see anyone on the ship. Roy didn't answer him. I guess he was in a state of shock. Josey and Paul were just dumbfounded!

"The ship stayed there, in a perfect picture, for two minutes and then started to fade. The bow started to disappear and a minute later the whole ship was gone."

I asked Buzz if he had any idea of what boat it might be.

"No," he said, "but it was a perfect stern-wheeler. And what amazed me at the time was the color. It was one flat color, sort of a sand color — the whole boat. I checked it out. The windows were all in it, the pilot house, a perfect steamboat! It looked like the boat had just had a 'prime coat.'"

Josephine broke in to say, "And the window frames were all painted dark brown."

Buzz continued: "I went out the next day in our boat, not saying why to anyone, and pulled in across at the point that juts out where we had seen the ship. I wanted to see. I *knew* there wouldn't be a mark, and there wasn't, but I had to take a look. You know, when they pull a riverboat up like that to pick up wood, they'd put the bow right into the sand so it's solid. The water was deep enough at that point where we saw the ship, for it to pull in for wood. It was one of the many wood stops in those days. We call it Fossil Point around here, because at one time there was a fossilized snail about fourteen inches in diameter in there — a huge fossilized snail — and some dummy had to go and try to take it out and broke it up!"

Buzz said it was not unusual at all to hear stories about ghost ships on the lake — that he had heard many and not paid any attention to them.

"But after seeing that one," he exclaimed, "my impression changed and I'm watching for one again! I'll never forget it! It was a perfect stern-wheeler, about the size of the *Klondike* (restored ship on the river bank in Whitehorse), and the *Klondike* was a big ship — the biggest — 1,226 tons. You know, there were two *Klondikes*. The first one sank near Hootalinqua (thirty miles down-river from Lake Laberge), and they salvaged just the engine and put it in *Klondike II*. Maybe, this phantom ship we saw was the original *Klondike!*

"Yeah," Buzz said quietly as he gazed out across the lake toward Fossil Point, "wouldn't *that* be something. I'm sure keeping my eyes peeled."

6

"KATE"   ~C. CADWELL

DAWSON CITY, YUKON

"Queen of the Klondike"
Kate Rockwell
of the
Palace Grand Theater

The Yukon River is a swift and unforgiving course of water that flows over three hundred fifty miles through mountain valleys north to Dawson City, Yukon Territory. The river angles west from there for eighteen hundred miles across Alaska, finally emptying into the Bering Sea. Beginning in the late 1890s, this river was navigated by mariners who piloted sturdy, twelve hundred ton wood-burning stern-wheelers around shifting sandbars and through dangerous rapids. The stern-wheelers carried food and supplies into the wilderness, as well as thousands of gold-hungry stampeders. Men and women, many without any moral conscience, were infected with a maniacal fever to strike it rich, any way possible.

In the minds of most, Dawson was the end of the agonizing hardships endured on the long journey north. For they had braved the treacherous trails over the snow-covered Coastal Mountain passes. Some, barely dressed for the sub-arctic temperatures, had dragged their supplies on home-made sleds or packed what they thought they would need on their backs. A well-known photographer made it through with his equipment loaded on a sled pulled by six goats.

The stampeders traveled five hundred miles to Dawson City from their starting points at Dyea and Skagway, Alaska. Left behind on the Chilkoot and White Pass trails were grim reminders of the sickening cruelty of their passing: wooden grave markers, carcasses of mules and horses, women's high button shoes, tins of food and rusting picks and shovels.

Upon reaching Lake Bennett on the other side of the mountains, these early argonauts built make-shift boats or rafts to cross the lakes that fed the upper Yukon. Stern-wheelers followed, connecting with the White Pass railroad, which was completed to Bennett in 1899. From its crude beginnings, an elaborate transportation system had been developed to deliver a new class of citizens to the "San Francisco of the North."

Many characters came to Dawson who later went on to fame and fortune. Jack London was a hopeful writer there during the gold rush. Robert Service arrived a little later as a bank teller, and the love of the Yukon in his blood was expressed eloquently in his celebrated poetry. Even Sid Grauman came to the wilds of the Klondike to try his luck digging for gold. But his theater in Hollywood was his richest find.

Walking the streets of Dawson today, one can very

74

easily leave present reality. You can hear heavy mining boots stomping the boardwalks. Honky tonk piano music drifts in the wind along with the throaty laughter of the dance hall girls as they entertain the wild and wooly men of old Dawson.

Many buildings of the old gold rush days have now been restored to their former glory. It's hard to separate yourself from the aura of past history, where fortunes were made and lost. These prospectors lived hard, worked hard and played hard. The Yukon winters were cold and unmerciful. Miners were happy to see the spring thaw so they could work the pay-dirt that had piled up during the winter.

Spring brought continuous daylight with warm winds. Everywhere the once-frozen ground sprang to life with brilliant flowers. White Yukon stars, blue lupines and scarlet fireweed. Birds of every description rode the boreal currents of air. Brown bear and grizzly brought their young to the edges of swiftly moving streams to feed on the salmon that fought their way through the rapids to spawn.

Along the quiet tributaries, prospectors worked their claims ten to twelve hours a day, shoveling gold-bearing gravel into hand-made sluice boxes. In the "Land of the Midnight Sun" long hours of daylight were put to good use.

However, neither the long workdays of summer, nor the sixty below zero temperatures of winter prevented the prospectors from seeking entertainment in the three big dance halls of the time. At the Savoy, which was later renamed the Palace

Grand, the miners crowded in to watch and listen to the most glamorous and highest paid entertainer of all in those days: Kathleen Rockwell, otherwise known as "Klondike Kate, Queen of the Yukon."

Kathleen Eloisa Rockwell was born in Junction City, Kansas on October 4, 1876 to Scotch-Irish parents. Her father, John W. Rockwell, was a telegraph operator, and her mother, Martha Alice Murphy, worked as a waitress. At the age of sixteen, Kate landed her first entertainment job as a chorus girl in New York. After receiving a letter from a girlfriend in Spokane, Washington, offering her a job in vaudeville, Kate headed west.

When the news of the Klondike gold strike reached Seattle and Spokane, Kate made up her mind to go north to Dawson City. A song and dance team was formed with three other entertainers, and they boarded a ship for Skagway, Alaska. By the time the weary group had climbed the Chilkoot and landed at Lake Bennett, all but Kate decided to back out of the deal. She was on her own.

Kate made it through to Whitehorse, where a letter waited for her offering a job with a big burlesque and musical comedy group that had formed in Victoria, British Columbia. The Savoy Theatrical Company would soon be the toast of Dawson, but Kate still had three hundred miles of Yukon River ahead of her.

The Northwest Mounted Police weren't letting women travel alone in the Yukon, so a determined Kate dodged the police by disguising herself as a boy.

She waited until a scow was about to pull out and jumped aboard, just as the lines came loose from the dock.

As Kate stepped onto shore in Dawson City, she was only slightly disillusioned that the streets were not paved with gold. Smiling bravely, she headed for the large theater building that was to be her home for many years. The Savoy would become the entertainment center of Dawson City, with Kate as the star.

The immense Savoy was lighted with coal-oil lamps and Kate would do her "cake-walk" wearing $1,500 gowns imported from Worth of Paris. This long-limbed beauty with reddish-gold hair electrified her audiences. Cheers would fill the hall, and miners threw gold nuggets at Kate as she gave them her sultry "come hither" smile. In the glow of the lamps her sensuous form moved across the stage. As she gracefully lifted her arms, billowing streams of multi-colored chiffon floated behind her.

On Christmas Eve in 1900, wild with the holiday spirit, the prospectors cut a crown from a tin can. On the jagged points they stuck lighted candles and crowned Kate, "Queen of the Klondike."

Unfortunately, some of the wax dripped into her hair and several candles fell, singeing her long curls. Very little ever slowed down this gutsy lady. She had her hair bobbed, which somehow added more glamor to her hauntingly beautiful face.

The large hall was heated with a red-hot potbellied stove. Outside the arctic winds howled, and the ground was frozen solid. But inside they were all a fun-loving, extraordinary mixture of humanity. Newly made millionaires, dance hall girls and gamblers. The hopeful, the successful and the forlorn, all coming together, celebrating as if tomorrow would never arrive.

Kate's loving heart and her devotion to helping others with sympathy, understanding and money, was her undoing. Her heartbreaking romance with Dawson bartender Alexander Pantages (whom she helped get started in the theater business), was to sadden her spirit for the rest of her life.

The couple left Dawson in 1901. Pantages fleeced Kate of thousands of dollars which he used to build a chain of movie and vaudeville houses in California. He later sold them for $3.5 million.

After years of treating Kate as his "sweetheart," Pantages threw her over for a younger woman. He married Lois Mendenhall, who was (as stated to Kate) "from the right side of the tracks."

Disillusioned and heartbroken, Kate started a suit against Pantages, seeking damages of $25,000. However, the case dragged on more than a year and she ended up with less than five thousand.

In June of 1929, Pantages' young wife was convicted of second degree manslaughter while driving in an intoxicated condition. Six people were injured and one person died as she sideswiped three cars and crashed into another.

Several months later, Pantages was arrested on a charge of assaulting a teenage girl who went to his office to get a job.

The fortune that Pantages had come by in such a heartless manner started to crumble.

It was rumored that when the prospectors heard what had happened to "their" Kate, they gathered together and set up Pantages by paying seventeen-year-old Eunice Pringle to stage the scene that was his downfall.

The Los Angeles Record of October 3, 1929 carried the following on page one: "We will show," said District Attorney Fitts to the jury, "that Pantages said, in substance, to Miss Pringle then, 'I want to talk to you about your act and I'm going to take you into my private office.'

"Pantages, in the words of Miss Pringle, 'went crazy' and put his left arm around her waist and his right hand over her mouth and began to kiss her, then bit her about the arms. Miss Pringle fought, but he kept his hand over her mouth and gradually forced her to the floor, where she lay kicking and struggling while on her back . . . ."

Kate returned to the Yukon and tried to lose herself in the life of the theater. But at that time, it still was a place of too many unhappy memories. She left again and settled in Medford, Oregon.

In 1933 Kate received a letter from Johnny Matson, a quiet Swedish prospector who had loved her since the first time he had seen her perform at the Savoy. After writing letters back and forth, they were married in Vancouver, British Columbia on July 14, 1933. Kate was fifty-seven and Matson was seventy.

Matson returned to Dawson and they both agreed that Kate should spend winters "outside." During the time that Kate was unable to make it to Dawson, they corresponded. In 1946, the letters from Matson stopped coming, and Kate began to worry. The Royal Canadian Mounted Police found Matson frozen to death seven miles from his cabin. Kate had him buried in his own "Yukon flower garden" and later had a prospector, Joe Sestak, mush in with a marker for her husband's grave.

The beloved "Queen of the Klondike" lived out her days in a modest but comfortable cottage outside of Sweethome, Oregon. She passed on in 1957 at the age of eighty with a trunk full of old memories.

From what I have been told, Kate's dauntless spirit had returned to the theater in Dawson that she loved so much.

Early in the summer of 1962, before work was started on the restoration of the Palace Grand, a young couple from Fairbanks found that they were not able to find a place to camp for the night in Dawson. It was pouring rain as they walked down King Street past the ruins of the once magnificent Savoy/Palace Grand theater. Thinking that no one would really care, they crawled under the old structure and found a dry place to roll out their sleeping bags for the night. Falling into an exhausted sleep, they were awakened an hour later by the sound of a woman weeping. The young man pulled a flashlight out of his backpack and searched among the broken boards and old theater furniture stored under the stage area, where they thought the sound came from, and found nothing.

Again they settled down to go to sleep, only to be awakened again to the sound of men and women laughing. This was followed by glass breaking and the music of an old honky-tonk piano.

Above the young couple, the rotting floor began to vibrate, and in one corner they could hear the ghostly whirring of an old roulette wheel.

Glancing at one another, they agreed without speaking that something unnatural was going on! Dragging their camping gear behind them, they crawled as fast as they could out from under the building onto the street. For a few moments they stood in the rain in front of the old theater looking back at where they had left the building. The only sound they could hear was the mewing of the gulls down near the river and a dog mournfully howling at the other end of town. It was four in the morning as they started off down the street, too frightened and wide awake to think about sleeping at all that night!

Later that summer, the reconstruction of the Palace Grand finally got underway. The old theater was completely torn down and an exact duplicate was built on the old foundations.

Shortly after the stage was finished, several of the carpenters and painters reported seeing "a very pretty lady" walking out onto the stage. She watched the workers for a few minutes and then "disappeared into thin air!" When asked what she looked like, one of the carpenters said to me, "Well, she sure had pretty red hair!"

Of all the stories I have been told concerning Kate's reappearance in the theater, the one that stands out the most was one related to me by Jane Olynyk, and I would like to pass it on to you exactly as she told it to me:

"Back in 1976 I was working for Parks Canada as a tour guide, taking people through the Palace Grand Theater. The experience I had was in August on a Monday night in 1976. I was tour-guiding and the theater was dark that night. We didn't have, at that time, a show on Monday nights. It was my job to make sure that everyone was out of the building so I could lock up.

"We used to take tours right up to the third floor where there were rooms that were used by the entertainers back in the old days, and one especially where Klondike Kate used to stay. That one room we had set aside and decorated to look exactly as it was when she stayed at the Palace Grand.

"I had gone up to the top floor and locked that room up along with all the others, and then went down to the main floor to check out the empty theater. Other people who worked in this place didn't like the job of turning off the lights. They thought it was kind of spooky, but it never bothered me. I had to go backstage and turn on the house lights to make sure that no one had wandered into the seating area.

So I went backstage, turned on the house lights and walked out onto the stage. I looked around to make sure the place was empty. On the second floor balcony on the left-hand side, in one of the boxes, there stood Kate! She was just standing there! It was rather strange and I wasn't frightened or anything, for I felt that there certainly wouldn't be anything frightening about Kate. I was rather calm actually. I knew instantly that it was her, for I had seen pictures of her doing what she called the 'veil dance,' where she had lots and lots of veils in different colors. Some of them were thirty feet long. And there she was, just standing there with her red hair and this gorgeous green gown. I could see her in color, but I could see through her, but there was color there. I could see the back wall through her. She was just slightly transparent but solid enough so that I knew it was her.

"I just stood there looking at her and then she started moving out of the box. I couldn't hear her but I knew that she was moving behind the boxes, and she came out of the royal box, which is second floor middle, and she walked right to the edge, looked at me again, smiled at me and then walked out again.

"I could hear the door back there close. I knew that all the doors were locked, so it was very strange. But I suppose not strange for a ghost.

"I felt very complimented after coming down from the stage. I have always had the feeling that she was in the theater watching us. And sometimes, when I showed the tourists her room, I could feel her there and it made me cry sometimes. There was such a presence or feeling of sorrow.. She was a very lonely lady. She had made so much money and then this scoundrel Pantages basically robbed her.

"She went south for a while after this business with Pantages, but the place that she was the happiest was here in Dawson City doing her shows. I don't know the reasons for her showing up in this theater, but I expect that because show business was her life, she just wanted to see that the shows continued.

"There are other people that have told me they have felt the presence of her here in the theater. Never did they have the feeling that it was a frightening experience, but one of gentleness, as if she had come here to where she was the happiest in her life.

"From that time on, when going up to her room, I always said, 'Goodnight, Kate!' I *had* to. Once you knew that she was clearly there, you just couldn't ignore her. As far as I am concerned, Kate has come home to where she was loved the most."

Jane Olynyk and her husband, Tom Naughten, have lived in Dawson City for more than ten years. Jane left her job as a tour guide after two years and was a social worker for Dawson City Health and Human Resources for nine years. She is now doing private consulting and working on her masters degree in psychology at the University of Columbia Pacific. Her husband is an archaeological research assistant for Canada Park Service.

7

85

"Ghostly Dog Team"

of the Klondike
Gold Fields

The following story was related to me by Dick North. Dick was a correspondent during the war in Vietnam and is one of the finest writers in the Yukon. Among the many of his published books are *The Mad Trapper of Rat River* and *The Lost Patrol.* He also has composed many other fine narratives about tremendously interesting incidents in the north country, especially with regard to his adventures in saving and restoring Jack London's cabin.

"There are plenty of mysteries and weird happenings in the long, frigid nights on the trail in the north country, when the temperatures range down to 65 and 70 below," expressed Dick, "a time when man and dog alike don't like to be traveling if they can help it."

An old prospector in Dawson City, who was from the Salcha area of Alaska, told Dick what happened to him:

"I was camped one night and my thermometer showed 72 below zero. The air was so still and quiet, you'd have thought you were an astronaut who had fallen out of his space capsule. My dogs were all bedded down for the night, though there had been some excitement earlier when Fagin, my lead dog, stole Henry the Eighth's chunk of dog salmon."

The prospector, being an ex-school teacher, liked to name his dogs after famous characters. He usually matched the character of the dog with the character of the story.

"Usually my dogs don't act up when the temperature is that low," the prospector continued, "but Fagin was the type who would swim through an open lead with the temperature 100 below if he thought he could steal an extra piece of grub!

"At any rate, the camp was quiet. There was no wind. The only noise was the occasional crackling of the fire, and soon that was frozen in silence. It was then it happened! A faint breeze sprang up, merely a wisp of air mind you, and then I saw a little picket of fog movin' up the creek toward the camp."

The prospector went on to say that he normally wasn't too concerned about such occurrences, but this little bank of fog moved like it had an entity all its own.

"About this time, Fagin, the lead dog, started whining and carrying on like he had been fed ling carcass (he didn't like ling), and then all the rest of the dogs started the same thing.

"Henry the Eighth was so scared by whatever it was that was coming up the trail, that he broke his chain and came over and tried to crawl into my bedroll with me! Now you try and keep a 150-pound Malamute from where he wants to go, and you have yourself quite a time!

"While I was busy holding Henry the Eighth out of my sleeping bag, the other dogs were diggin' for China and that fog bank came right up over us and kept on going!"

The prospector went on to say that he felt a clammy feeling as the fog went past, not unlike the air of the sea. Along with that, he said there was a faint creaking that a sled makes as it races through the snow.

"It was the weirdest feeling I have ever experienced," he said. "The dogs dug so deep and so far into the snow, you'd have thought a rotary plow had hit the area! I couldn't even get Fagin to come out of his hole for prime dog salmon. And if Fagin refuses his favorite food, you *knew* there had to be something wrong!

"Need I tell you, I got that fire going again and sat up the rest of the night just mulling this over in my head. By morning (as much of a morning we have up here this time of year), the dogs had quieted down somewhat. And I'll tell you, I was glad to head away from that place, and I don't think you'll catch me there again!"

What was it then that came up the trail? Was it a phantom dog team driven by a man who has long since gone to his reward? Or was it merely a passing wolf? Only Fagin and Henry the Eighth and the other dogs could have explained the mystery, and they too are long gone now.

8

"John Stockton"

The Perpetual
Prospector on
Glacier Creek

One frigid Yukon winter afternoon, my friend Jackson and I sat in the living room of her peaceful, warm little log cabin and discussed ghosts and other hauntings.

The fire in the wood stove crackled. Several of her seven Siamese cats slept on colorful patchwork pillows, tucked here and there in corners. Others draped themselves over the edge of the loft, watching us with half-closed eyes.

Over steaming cups of coffee and buttered Bannock, fresh from the oven, we talked about one ghost in particular, John Stockton.

Just before I left, Jackson handed me a hand-drawn map of a mining claim, far to the north, outside of Dawson City.

"I want you to go up there when the weather breaks and take a look at John's grave site," Jackson said. "The miners say they have seen him watching their gold operations from the hill above, where his grave is located. I worked there at the mine as a camp cook several years ago, and I have seen him too!"

I folded the map, tucked it safely in my pocket and later called my sister Fran up in Anchorage, Alaska. She had shared many of my adventures. Perhaps she would like to go on this one as well.

In June of 1987, after the spring thaw, Fran and I headed north some 350 miles up the road to Dawson City, Yukon. The trusty van was loaded with camping gear and all the necessary things we would need for roughing it back in the mountains near Glacier Creek, at a place called Sixty Mile.

Sixty Mile had been at one time a rough and bustling camp of more than two thousand gold seekers. Today, all that remains are three log cabins in fairly decent shape and an old dredge. One of the cabins is inhabited by a rather reclusive prospector, an Englishman by the name of Jimmy Lynch. Jimmy must have been around 65 years old when we met him. He quietly worked what was known as the Discovery Claim.

To get to Sixty Mile we had to go west from Dawson City over the Top of the World Highway. Leaving Dawson we crossed the Yukon River on a small ferry and then headed in that direction. Our van hummed along over the rather narrow, two-lane gravel road which wound and curved, ever higher, through ancient rounded mountains, crested here and there with strange rocky outcroppings called erosion pillars. Finally, there were no trees at all. The dwarfish spruce trees had been left behind, and we were beginning to feel that "Top of the World" was an apt description.

Even though a car or truck would pass us occasionally, it was a strange and lonely feeling, gazing out over the seemingly endless miles of arctic tundra, now beginning to blossom with blue lupines and white-tufted cotton grass. The stillness was interrupted once in a while by the shrill whistle of a hoary marmot. This was primeval earth and we were caught in a moment of geological time — alone in the wilderness.

Driving on, we spotted a crumbling log cabin close to the road. According to Jackson's map, this was a "marker," and shortly after that we turned off onto an even narrower road, heading down the mountains in the direction of Sixty Mile. We blessed the brakes and gritted our teeth as our van bounced from one hardened muddy rut to the other — over the rocks, around sharp curves and down steep, graveled grades. At last we came to a level, grass-covered clearing, through which ran a swift, beautifully clear mountain stream. On the left of us, tucked in among the trees were three comfortable-looking old log cabins. In a branch of the creek, straight ahead of us, like a towering, rusty metal dinosaur, sat a time-weathered dredge. Hovering over it were graceful, protecting aspens. Sixty Mile at last!

According to the map, we were to turn to our right and cross the stream. One problem: no bridge! We could see from faint tracks that other vehicles had crossed here — no doubt four-wheel drives and Caterpillar tractors. But a *loaded* van? First we got out of the van to look at the depth of the water to find the highest point. Back in the van, we looked at each other and said, "Okay, let's back up and make a run for it!" Needless to say, the nearest towing garage was too far away to give us help if we made a mistake. Gunning the engine, we pointed the nose of the van in the direction of a single lane road across the stream.

Once on the other side of the water, Fran patted the dashboard lovingly and whispered, "thank you!" We always talk to our cars, don't you? Especially in the far north.

At this point we were getting rather nervous. Not about the narrow road that curved in and around mounds of tailings piled high and left there from old mining operations, but about a law that we had heard about. This law, we were told, states that you don't encroach upon anyone's mining claim without permission from the owner. Were we going to be met with shotguns? All we were looking for was a ghost!

Fran looked at me and said, "Well, here's hoping they are friendly!" And we drove on.

I should say we crept on, because there were places where only a mountain goat would take a chance crossing. At one tight spot, we certainly thought the van would tip over and slide into the stream below.

After heading around one more hill of tailings, we saw a modern mining camp ahead of us. Two big white construction trailers were tucked against the side of the hill across the stream. Wow, civilization!

Enormous bulldozers were working the stream and a huge mechanical sluice box angled down into the water, with one end high atop a pile of tailings.

Working the equipment were three big men in hard hats, t-shirts and blue jeans.

When they saw us stopped near the edge of the stream, one of them walked over with a scowl on his face (hopefully from the bright sunlight) and said in a rather gruff voice, "What can we do for you ladies?"

We cautiously got out of the van and I handed him the map.

"We're looking for a haunted grave site," I said.

His face broke into a wide grin, and he said, "Oh, you mean *John*! He's up there."

He pointed to the mountainside above the stream, and then extended his hand.

"I'm Dan Chuvas," he said jovially. "My wife Peggy is up there in the trailer. She can tell you all about John."

Both Fran and I were puzzled with Dan's nonchalant manner at the mention of a haunted grave site. Was he making fun of us? Not *hardly*, we found out later.

Starting the van, we inched carefully across a single-lane wooden plank bridge and parked next to one of the large trailers. When we knocked on the door, a hesitant voice said, "Yes?" Through the half-open door we introduced ourselves and told her what we were looking for. Peggy opened the door with a big smile. She was a small young woman with short dark hair and looked more like she belonged on the beach at Malibu, rather than in the wilds of a northern mining camp. What a pretty lady! After looking at the kitchen table, we readily understood why she was cautious about opening the door. She had been measuring and weighing gold flakes and large nuggets! I'm sure my mouth must have dropped open. I'd never seen such a sight in all my life!

Seated in their comfortable living room, Peggy, Fran and I talked for what seemed like hours about John Stockton. And later, over dinner, the men willingly told us more about this extremely interesting and rather lonely ghost.

John Stockton was born in 1865 and died near his claim in 1944 at the age of 79. At this writing, I have not been able to find out if he had any living relatives. The Northwest Mounted Police and friends in the area buried John on his gold claim. It was a site that he had selected himself near two beautiful trees on the edge of the hill overlooking the Sixty Mile valley.

John was 44 years old when he filed his first gold claim in 1909. No one could tell me how long he had been in the Yukon, but according to copies of his applications for placer mining that I was able to obtain, he filed his first claim at the mouth of Big Gold Creek on April 20, 1909. The last claim he filed was on December 29, 1916 at Glacier Creek. He filed six claims altogether over a period of seven years.

Let's go back in history a little and get some idea why these prospectors hung on to their claims and guarded them with such tenacity — and in John's case, even after the death of his physical body.

As early as 1892, men were finding their fortunes in the mountain valleys near Glacier Creek, sixty miles west of Dawson. Three creeks — Miller, Big Gold and Glacier — were originally worked by four men: Nolasque Tremblay, Joe Lemay, Joe Roi (King) and Louis Boucher. In 1892, these men and others took out more than $6,000 in gold from the Sixty Mile valley, and much more followed in the years ahead. Between 1892 and 1896, $282,000 worth of gold was found in the Sixty Mile area.

In 1896, Robert Henderson found gold on one of the six tributaries of the Klondike River. He mentioned his find to George Washington Carmack, a Californian who had come to the Yukon in the 1880s and had married the daughter of a Tagish chief. Accompanied by his wife, Kate, and two brothers-in-law, Skookum Jim and Dawson Charlie, Carmack had been looking for gold in the same area as Henderson. However, Carmack had been nicknamed "Siwash George" by unkind white prospectors, and Henderson did not want any Indians to benefit from his discovery. So Carmack and his party decided to explore another valley, and on August 17, 1896 they struck gold on Rabbit Creek. So rich was the find that Carmack supposedly said the gold lay on the creek bottom "like cheese in a sandwich." The creek soon became known as Bonanza.

Word of the big Klondike strike spread like wildfire to Sixty Mile and other Yukon River settlements. Many of the prospectors left for Dawson City to hit what they thought would be rich "paydirt," only to find that most of the good claims were already taken. However, many of the early Yukon miners were able to stake claims in

1896 and 1897.

News of the gold discovery was slow reaching the outside world until the *SS Portland* steamed into Seattle on July 17, 1897 with its famous "ton of gold." The rush was on!

Two days later, the mail steamer *Queen* sailed north with the first load of stampeders. Many thousands would follow to the small homestead ports of Skagway and nearby Dyea, the gateways to the White Pass and Chilkoot trails. After landing on the beach, these would-be prospectors had a tortuous struggle ahead of them over these mountain passes. Very little marked the trails, and travel entailed perilous switchbacks along mountainsides and through canyons. In the winter they had huge snow fields to cross. Many men and women lost their lives in a terrible snowslide on the Chilkoot in the spring of 1898, and thousands of horses perished on the White Pass.

The trails converged about 40 miles inland at Lake Bennett, one of the headwaters of the Yukon River. The stampeders waited there for the ice to go out and built boats for the rest of the journey, approximately 450 miles downriver to the gold fields. At the confluence of the Yukon and Klondike rivers, Dawson City sprang up. By the summer of 1898, Dawson was a swarming mass of humanity, all feverishly seeking their golden fortune.

And where was John Stockton in this whole picture?

Sixty Mile had been a bustling gold camp,

complete with a large general store. Jimmy Lynch at Sixty Mile showed us an old ledger someone had given him from the general store, which no longer existed. He told us that it had been bulldozed over many years ago. But in this ledger we found an entry: "John Stockton — one pound of tea, 50 cents; one pair of gloves, 15 cents." From these two things and the records of John filing six claims along the streams, we knew that he was not the figment of someone's imagination, or a cruel hoax on the part of intoxicated people in Dawson saloons.

Miners are a strange breed of people. They keep pretty much to themselves. Of course, there are exceptions to the rule, but most of them are loners. They work up there from sunup to sundown. The Klondike summers are short, but the days are long. In a twenty-four-hour period the "midnight sun" hovers in twilight between ten at night until about two in the morning.

Jimmy Lynch told us that he remembered John Stockton, but, as a young boy, he very rarely saw him. Jimmy said he would run into John on the trail once in a while. He would speak to him, and John would say quietly, "Good morning" and disappear into the hills. At 17, Jimmy went off to war. When he came back around 1944-45, he was told that John was dead and buried on the hill.

We were told where John's cabin was located, but we never could find it. Like many of the cabins built back then, it too had succumbed to the forces of nature.

After 1944, John's claims were bought by Manfred Peschke of Whitehorse, and he is still mining around the area of John's grave. From what we saw when we were there, the mining operations sort of gave wide berth to that little hill.

But stories of a "spectre" on the hillside near Glacier Creek slowly filtered out of Sixty Mile and were discussed with casual interest in the various meeting places up and down the Yukon River. Ghost stories were not unusual in the Klondike. It was said that anyone who dared stake a claim on John's property had so much trouble that they had to "pack it in" and leave to mine further down the stream.

Al Downes of Whitehorse told me a story about a Frenchman who worked on John's claim. After a month or so, he finally gave up and left the mining operation at three in the morning without saying a word to anyone. Some said that he was scared witless by an apparition that flew through the air wrapped in an old blanket, and he was sure this must be John. For it was said that when John died, he was just wrapped in a blanket and buried only two feet down in the ground.

No wonder the gravesite is covered with a large mound of rocks. Perhaps someone thought that John's body needed weighting down. Knowing what the weather is like up there in October, perhaps the ground was too frozen to be able to dig any deeper.

In 1980, Jim Ostrowalker (now of Vancouver, B.C., Canada) started working John's claim along with two other men by the names of Eric and Barney.

Ostrowalker told me that when he first saw John's grave, it had been terribly defaced. He fixed the cross that had been knocked down and brightened up the faded lettering: "John Stockton 1865-1944."

The mining company had been running two shifts. They were stripping the ground with bulldozers near John's grave in preparation for mining, and they very seldom ever gave serious thought to what happened to the grave. Numerous times the other men would back over the site with their equipment. Ostrowalker finally placed a large mound of rocks over the grave.

Shortly after the operations started, trouble began. The nightshift men would place their lunch pails down in certain places, and when they returned, the lunches were gone. Mudholes would appear where, a short time before, the ground had been bone dry. Parts disappeared from big tractors, or they would become mired down in the mudholes.

Then it started to rain, just over the site, every day at three o'clock sharp! Two of the nightshift men asked to be put on days. When they were refused, they quit their jobs.

The men who owned the mining company couldn't keep up with the problems, so they pulled out of the claim and decided to work further down Glacier Creek. Ostrowalker told me that he went back up to the claim to retrieve his backhoe, and the tire was flat. It hadn't been before he left.

He said he finally sat down next to John's grave and talked to him.

"This isn't the kind of help I need, John!"

Ostrowalker said.

He got up and went back to his machine, and the tire was no longer flat. He was the only man on the hill, and he could see his backhoe from the grave site.

As Ostrowalker told me, "After we pulled out of the site, we didn't have any more problems. It's too bad that the claim can't be worked. There's good gold there, but we can't recover any of it at all without being plagued with problems. Especially that weird rain. By the way, it hasn't rained up there since we left the hill."

He said that he had seen John standing on the hill by his grave site at least fifty or sixty times during the summer. Ostrowalker would look up the hill near the old air strip, and there John would be, standing in plain sight, just watching what the men were doing at the new mining operations.

Ostrowalker went on to say, "Just before we left Sixty Mile in the fall, I went up again to John's grave and rebuilt the rock mound once more and placed fireweed flowers in front of the cross and said my goodbyes. Dan and Peggy Chuvas took over the operation from us."

In the quiet of Dan and Peggy's living room, we were told about the things that had happened in their camp. Even though John's grave was across Glacier Creek from them and up on the hill, they felt that he wandered into their camp once in a while. Peggy said that she would take a walk, not far from their trailers, and feel someone behind her. Looking back, she saw no one there, and all the men were down on the creek mining.

One of the men said that one day he was in the main trailer, and he could hear the kitchen cupboard doors opening and closing. He thought one of the other men was there, and called out. No one answered. Later he confronted the other men about it, and they had been in the bunkhouse at the time, sound asleep.

Peggy said that on another day she carefully covered a cake with plastic wrap and went outside. When she returned, the cake had been uncovered in a very tidy way. It couldn't have been animals. The door was closed, no one had been in the kitchen, and the whole crew was in the creek working.

Every once in a while, the men look up from the creek and see John watching them from the hill. They wave to him. They also make sure no one touches his grave, and they check it at times to see if it is still in good shape. They all seem to have such respect for John. They even rolled high, heavy metal drain pipes across the trail to the site. Never will a bulldozer, or anyone, disturb John Stockton's resting place again.

My sister Fran and I drove up the steep hill. We parked the van on the old air strip, now covered with an immense carpet of newly blossoming fireweed, and walked back to the grave. We tidied up the rocks surrounding the white wooden cross, and said hello to John. I told him that I was trying to write a story about him and seemed to be running into problems with regard to information about his life.

Later that night, after a great dinner of barbecue chicken at Chuvas's camp, I took a walk along the creek.

Looking up at John's grave among the trees, I said outloud, "What do I have to do to find out more about you, John?"

And a voice said, *"Leave me alone!"*

I turned and no one was there.

True to his nature, John remains a friend to miners, but has no time for curiosity seekers!

Afterword

A number of people have asked me why I wrote a book about ghosts. Without going into a long dissertation about my personal beliefs, I will say to begin with that I sincerely believe there are such things as ghosts. That ghosts are spirits and are a normal continuation of our energy. As I have said in this book, "We are energy, and we are forever."

Most of what we consider unnatural is merely something that we cannot totally understand. As the astronaut Captain Edgar Mitchell once said, "There is no such thing as supernatural. Everything is natural."

Down through the years, we have been led to believe that ghosts go around clanking chains and moaning and are there to scare you witless. I'm not saying that meeting a ghost is not a frightening experience, but only because we do not understand what is happening. Nor do we understand *why* these things happen. I think that our understanding should start with learning more about life after death. Or as some people say, "life after life" or "life and rebirth."

If we believe that our souls or spirits just lie down and die along with our physical bodies, and that's the end of if all, then we are in serious trouble. We *do* go on from this plane of life to something or somewhere else. And when we go, we leave imprints behind — not just in memories but on the very ether that surrounds us all. Wherever we go from here, there are times, I'm sure, when we are able to make contact for various reasons — perhaps because of things that have been left undone that are extremely important.

When someone close to you has left his or her physical body and gone on, have you ever said to yourself, "I wish I had done more for him/her," or "I wish I had said 'I love you' more often?" Who is to say that they might wish the same thing?

Collecting ghost stories was rather difficult in some respects. I had to cover a lot of territory. And in the north that sometimes means hundreds of miles — a lot of it over pretty rough terrain. Hunting for factual material to back up some of these stories — such as birth and death records, copies of mine claims, old ledgers, geological survey maps, history books, old newspapers, funeral records, land titles, and so forth — was a real challenge. Not forgetting flat tires, broken springs, mosquitos, sore feet, rain, and rocks under our sleeping bags. But it was a lot of fun, really!

It was also hard to get most people to talk about their experiences. And yet there were some who were willing to "tell all." People would hesitate because they didn't want others to think they were "off their rocker," and they would say to me, "Please don't use my real name." Certainly I wouldn't do this if they felt uncomfortable about discussing their unusual occurrence.

Remembering my experiences over the past thirty years, I can certainly relate to this. I have been called a "nut" more times than I care to remember. So, I have to remind myself that being called a "nut," or just plain "weird," is much better than being called boring!

To me, gathering these stories was a marvelous adventure. I met some of the most wonderful people whom I have ever known — and many of them in some strange, out-of-the-way places. I felt a kinship to many of them. Here were normal human beings who had had the opportunity to see "beyond the veil." Who knew that there is more to us than meets the eye. Here were people who could pinch the flesh of their bodies and know that when that flesh disappeared into dust, the real person moved on to another great adventure.

Also, writing about ghosts helped *me* understand more about who we are and where we go from here, even though I had delved into these things for many years.

The Yukon and Alaska have always attracted strong personalities. And some of them refuse to leave, even after death!

I sincerely hope that you enjoyed these stories as much — if not more — than I did putting them together. And there are more to come!

If any of you who are reading this would care to get in touch with me regarding your own experiences with a "ghost of the north," please write me care of the publishers, and they will forward your letters on to me.

Many thanks to all of you who trusted me with your "ghostly experiences" and made this first book possible.

— *Shirley Jonas*

SOURCES

Libraries and Archives
Klondike Gold Rush National Historical Park Library - Skagway, Alaska - Frank Norris, historian.
Portland Oregonian archives
Whitehorse Star archives

Unpublished Material
Bolton, Dee. "The Ghost of the Golden North." Paper about March 30, 1975 seance.

Government Documents
Alaska First Judicial District court records and deeds, Skagway, Alaska magistrate's office.
Cockfield, W.E. Memoir No. 123 for Canada Department of Mines Geological Survey: Sixty Mile and Ladue Rivers Area - Yukon, 1921.

Bibliography
Berton, Pierre. "The Klondike Fever." New York: Alfred A. Knopf, 1958.
Clifford, Howard. "The Skagway Story." Seattle: Alaska Northwest, 1975.
Cohen, Stan. "Yukon River Steamboats." Missoula: Pictorial Histories, 1982.
DeArmond, R.N., ed. "Klondike Newsman: Stroller White." Skagway: Lynn Canal, 1990.
Lucia, Ellis. "Klondike Kate." Sausalito: Comstock, 1962.

ABOUT THE AUTHOR

Born and raised in Michigan, Shirley Jonas was the founder and director of Michigan ESP Research Associates Foundation and has done thirty years of research in the field of the paranormal. Shirley and her late husband Bert spent more than ten years in the Yukon and Alaska and made their home in the historic port of Skagway. Shirley now takes care of her "critters" in northern Michigan and plans to return to Alaska and the Yukon to research more ghosts.

AND THE ILLUSTRATOR

Chris Caldwell has been drawing the people of the North since settling in the Yukon in 1979. A self-taught artist from Winnipeg, Caldwell held her first exhibition at the Yukon Gallery in 1983 and has since commissioned numerous oils, portraits, prints, brochure covers, pins, maps, t-shirts, or "Christmas card critters." Her popular "Bush Panic" series in the *Whitehorse Star* has been collected in two books. Caldwell's sense of humor is as much a trademark as her fondness for donning a ten-gallon hat and climbing onto a horse. The ideas for many of her works are rooted in personal experiences, such as getting together with her friend Shirley Jonas and talking about ghosts. Caldwell recently moved with her family to Kenai, Alaska.

If you would like to order more copies
of this book or obtain a list
of other gold rush titles,
please contact:

LYNN CANAL PUBLISHING
P.O. Box 1898, 264 Broadway
Skagway, Alaska 99840-0498
Phone 907-983-2354